Strategic Studies Institute Monograph

PERSPECTIVES ON RUSSIAN FOREIGN POLICY

Stephen J. Blank
Editor

September 2012

*****

ii

CONTENTS

Foreword v

1. Defying That Sinking Feeling:
   Russia Seeks to Uphold Its Role
   in the Multistructural International
   System in Flux 1
   Pavel K. Baev

2. The Sacred Monster: Russia
   as a Foreign Policy Actor 25
   Stephen J. Blank

3. Ideology and Soft Power
   in Contemporary Russia 195
   Ariel Cohen

About the Contributors 215

FOREWORD

The essays collected in this volume comprise a panel on Russian foreign policy that was presented at the Strategic Studies Institute's (SSI) annual Conference on Russia on September 26-27, 2011, held at Carlisle, PA. These chapters aimed at analyzing not just the day to day diplomacy, but some of the deeper structures of Russian foreign policy, both their material basis in actual policy and the cognitive structures or mentality that underlies it. This issue is now more important with the return of Vladimir Putin to the presidency of Russia and the fact that major transformations in international relations are occurring today across the globe and at an unprecedented pace.

The assessment of such changes, and of governments' policy responses to them, lies at the heart of any effort to conceive of a strategy that makes sense in today's world. Without some viable sense of trends and of the forces that shape key actors' strategies and policies (which are decidedly not the same thing), no government can navigate safely through the shoals of contemporary world politics or make informed judgments concerning war and/or peace. Since both war and politics are interactive processes "where the enemy gets a vote," a profound grasp of global political and economic trends is essential to the formulation of sound U.S. policies and strategies, especially as regards so important an actor as the Russian Federation.

Providing such informed strategic analysis is SSI's primary function. Such analytical efforts constitute the bedrock of its activities and of its responsibilities to its audience. Accordingly, we are happy to present this volume to our readers in the belief that it will contribute substantially to their understanding of the contemporary world and help them to make the informed judgments about U.S. interests, policies, and strategy.

Douglas C. Lovelace

DOUGLAS C. LOVELACE, JR.
Director
Strategic Studies Institute

CHAPTER 1

DEFYING THAT SINKING FEELING: RUSSIA SEEKS TO UPHOLD ITS ROLE IN THE MULTISTRUCTURAL INTERNATIONAL SYSTEM IN FLUX

Pavel K. Baev

INTRODUCTION

The economic and political turmoil of the year 2011 has shown that the ever-evolving international system is growing rapidly in complexity and generates challenges that not only catch the policymakers by surprise, but also exceed their ability to produce adequate answers. Russia is struggling to adjust to these accelerating power shifts while also sinking into its own crisis of governance driven by the exhaustion of the economic model based on redistribution of expanding petro-revenues.[1] As its domestic politics are based on preserving stability that is eroded by systemic corruption and accumulating discontent, so, too, its foreign policy aims at upholding the role of a major power that is not supported by sufficient resources. In both domains, the Russian leadership, which now has to go through another round of self-reformatting, typically remains in denial of the weakness of its control over the game-changing developments but demonstrates high ambitions for staying in charge of the rules.

In the period of increasing self-assertiveness in the mid-2000s, the rather simplistic worldview prevalent in the Moscow political elite was shaped by the concept of multipolarity, which essentially predicted an unraveling of the unfair and unnatural U.S. dominance on the global arena.[2] This proposition is omitted in the 2008 Foreign Policy Concept (which also does not mention Russia's status as a Great Power), but just a month after its approval, President Dmitri Medvedev formulated five principles of Russian foreign policy, and the second one asserts that:

> The world should be multi-polar. A single-pole world is unacceptable. Domination is something we cannot allow. We cannot accept a world order in which one country makes all the decisions, even as serious and influential a country as the United States of America. Such a world is unstable and threatened by conflict.[3]

The economic recession that originated in the subprime U.S. debt crisis in the autumn of 2007 was initially seen in Moscow as a manifestation of multipolarity, but in late 2008, the Russian economy experienced a contraction of such depth that foreign policy thinking lost any coherence. The proud feeling of a rising power that has every right to demand respect from declining peers has suddenly changed into a sinking feeling accentuated by unavoidable reflections on the collapse of the Union of Soviet Socialist Republics (USSR) 20 years ago. The scheme of multipolarity has been put aside as much too simplistic but in its stead nothing more sophisticated was adopted, so the current big picture, as seen from Moscow, comes out as an eclectic mix of residual great-power ambitions, intrinsic anti-Americanism, wishful thinking about the golden age of gas, and shallow hopes to retain the privileges granted to Russia by international law.[4] This chapter does not sort out this discord and cacophony, but attempts to evaluate the implications of compulsive attempts to punch above its weight by looking into the nuclear domain, the hard power-centered geopolitical interactions, the economic relations, and the workings of international institutions.

STRUGGLING TO PRESERVE THE NUCLEAR BIPOLARITY

With all the revolutionary changes of the last 20 years in the symbolically rather than practically important area of nuclear armaments, the world system remains essentially bipolar because the U.S. and Russian strategic arsenals exceed those of three other legitimate nuclear powers—China, France, and the United Kingdom (UK)—by an order of magnitude. Russia attaches pivotal importance to preserving this inherited status, which involves pursuing the unattainable goal of maintaining a strategic parity. The prime value for Moscow of the reset process initiated by U.S. President Barack Obama in the spring of 2009 is in formally fixing this parity in the legally binding Prague Treaty, and that largely explains the exhaustion on this process after the miraculous ratification in December 2010. The built-in paradox of this achievement is that Russia insisted on fixing the quantitative ceiling of this parity rather high, so that its superiority over other nuclear powers would be in no doubt, but it cannot sustain any leg of its strategic triad at the prescribed level.[5] Far greater investments than in the United States are channeled into the programs for deploying new generations of sea-launched ballistic missiles (SLBMs) and intercontinental ballistic missiles (ICBMs), yet the rate of decommissioning the missiles that are past the expiration date—and in the near future, long-range bombers as well—is so high that the aggregate number is fast going down, which is never acknowledged in the official discourse.[6]

Russian concerns about preserving a semblance of strategic parity are exacerbated by U.S. plans for building a missile defense system, which is seen as a means to render the whole system of nuclear checks and balances irrelevant. The main focus of controversy is currently the North Atlantic Treaty Organization (NATO) commitment to deploying a European anti-ballistic missile (ABM) system, and while the intensity of Moscow's objections might appear seriously exaggerated, in fact, through this intransigence the Russian leadership seeks to exploit the questionable readiness of many European states to invest in radars and interceptors in a time of severe budget cuts.[7] At the same time, Russia prioritizes the deployment of a new generation of surface-to-air missiles (the S-400 and S-500 systems) and the integration of various assets into an air-space defense system, which is a dubious proposition given the record of failures with space launches.[8]

The desire to preserve the status and the privileges of a nuclear superpower is the main driver of Russia's long-set course on preventing other states from acquiring these weapons; however, its nonproliferation policy is not without ambiguity. Proliferation of weapons of mass destruction (WMDs) and missile technologies is defined as one of the military risks in the 2010 edition of the *Russian Military Doctrine* (along with the aspiration to move NATO's infrastructure to Russia's neighborhood and the deployment of an anti-missile system), but there is an underlying question in this assessment about whether a possible appearance of several newly-nuclearized states could make Russia's massive arsenal more politically prominent.[9] In the crucial case of Iran, Moscow did agree on introducing limited United Nations (UN) sanctions but has indicated that it is not prepared to go any further along this road, generally perceiving the very probable acquisition by Tehran of several nuclear warheads as an unfortunate development, but one that by no means constitutes a direct threat to Russia.[10] Nonproliferation considerations are only a minor limitation in the aggressive policy of exporting Russian nuclear technologies, for which the *Rosatom* is relying on state support for expanding into new markets such as Turkey or Vietnam and potentially the Gulf monarchies.[11]

Grave risks involved in maintaining the resource-consuming and partially obsolete nuclear complex do not compel the Russian leadership to share the vision of a nuclear-free world rejuvenated by President Obama. Paying appropriate lip-service to this far-fetched proposition Medvedev actually presides over the most determined effort to modernize nuclear assets, which are seen as crucial for national security and hugely valuable for political prestige. One manifestation of this increasing reliance on nuclear instruments is a pronounced reluctance to engage in any negotiations on reducing the nonstrategic (tactical) nuclear weapons in Europe or even to allow a modicum of transparency for this arsenal, which quite possibly stores more warheads than the strategic forces.[12] The problem with the policy of upholding the position of the second nuclear super-power is that it consolidates the material basis of bilateral confrontation, so the best reset intentions cannot overcome the traditional deadlock of deterrence.[13] In the opinion of the Russian leadership, the respect coming from the privilege of being a major strategic adversary for the United States more than compensates for the lost opportunities that could have been gained through entering the crowded marketplace of U.S. allies.

MANEUVERING IN THE GEOPOLITICAL MULTIPOLARITY

The construction of nuclear balances occurs in a reality that in many ways is virtual (despite the physical reality of nuclear weapons), while in the real world, as seen from the prevalent Russian worldview, states compete for advancing their national interests relying primarily on their hard power, the core of which is made up of conventional military capabilities. Despite U.S. superiority in the most modern elements of these capabilities, its ability to project power is seriously limited, as the wars in Iraq and Afghanistan have brutally confirmed, so the Realpolitik world is effectively and increasingly multipolar. A large part of the Russian political elite originating in various power structures (first of all, the Russian Secret Police (KGB)/Russian Federal Security Service (FSB) superstructure) instinctively rather than theoretically tend to interpret international relations as essentially geopolitical.[14] In this perspective, Russia must constantly assert its position as a major and independent power-pole checking and pre-empting encroachments from all directions on its natural sphere of influence, which does not necessarily coincide with the borders of the former USSR.[15]

A key assumption in this defensive geopolitics is about the inherent hostility of the West, and that makes NATO into the main antagonist, which has to be contained from advancing eastward so that the first and the most specific military risk defined by the 2010 *Military Doctrine* would be neutralized.[16] Partnership with NATO could only be a means towards this end, and the recommendations of some liberal think-tanks to President Dmitri Medvedev to aim at membership in the Alliance amounts to malignant wishful thinking.[17] Russia would not have been able to withstand the drive of the NATO military machine, but it has enjoyed a run of good fortune because the unity of the Alliance has been deeply damaged by U.S. intervention in Iraq, and the war in Afghanistan continues to drain resources from the armed forces of key member-states while heading towards the inescapable defeat.[18] The intervention in Libya, which has caused some misgivings among the Russian leadership, has also added to the NATO crisis by exposing the decline of its power-projecting capabilities and leading to an outcome that may be very far from the desired one.[19] Severe cuts in the defense budgets of major European states, executed despite the needs revealed by the Libyan intervention, are interpreted in Moscow as favorable changes that reduce the risks emanating from NATO.[20]

The only real security guarantee in the Realpolitik world can be provided by one's own hard power, and the military reform abruptly launched in the autumn of 2008 was supposed to gain Russia usable instruments for the period when the United States and NATO remain entangled in the two unwinnable wars. The reform was long-overdue, but it is hard to imagine a less fortunate moment to start radical restructuring and downsizing than during the tumble down into an unexpected severe economic crisis. Defense Minister Anatoly Serdyukov deserves credit for his stubborn determination in executing the reform plan, but his complete ignorance of military-organizational and strategic matters necessitated severe purges in the High Command and resulted in a profound deterioration of combat capability, first of all in the Ground Forces.[21] The crucial issue of conscription is in limbo, and the main controversy thickens currently around the viability of the recently approved rearmament program that aims ambitiously at replacing the whole arsenal of aging Soviet weapons but boldly ignores financial realities.[22] In fact, many yawning deficiencies, particularly in command, control, communications, and intelligence (C^3I) systems, could only be eliminated by importing technologies or full sets of equipment from the West, which requires a new level of partnership with NATO.[23]

The impossible question for NATO in this cooperation is about where and to what political ends the modernized and upgraded Russian armed forces would be used. Geopolitical fantasies provide few clues about it; for that matter, the withdrawal of U.S. troops from Afghanistan could result in a destabilization of Central Asia, but Russia would hardly take on the role of security provided (as it did in Tajikistan in the early 1990s), exactly because this region is no longer seen as a frontier of geopolitical competition. Much speculation has been fueled by the geopolitical struggle for the Arctic, but Moscow has discovered that its military position of strength, even if augmented with a couple of specially trained brigades, generates few political dividends, and so Russia opts for a cooperative policy, confirming this choice by the new border treaty with Norway, which is far from popular with public opinion.[24] One region where Russia is keen to put its military might into play is the Caucasus, but here its main security challenge is the smoldering civil war in the North Caucasus, which the neighbors and competitors are careful not to fan, but Moscow still fails to extinguish.[25] In geopolitical terms, the most unstable power imbalance has emerged in the Far East, but Russia has no answer to the staggering rise of China and so prefers to pretend that the ambivalent strategic partnership is on a solid footing, ignoring its obvious inability to develop and defend Russia's vast Pacific periphery.

FALLING BEHIND IN ECONOMIC GLOBALIZATION

Political thinking in Russia is increasingly econo-mized and even mercantilized, and from a strictly business perspective, the scheme of multipolarity is only of limited relevance since nonstate actors pursue their profits with little regard to state interests. The rather unsophisticated self-descriptions of Russia as the energy superpower typical for the mid-2000s did not survive the economic contraction at the end of the decade, not only because of the sharp but short fall in oil prices, but primarily because the vulnerability of the position of raw materials supplier (or appendage as the Soviet propaganda used to define it) became too obvious.[26] Medvedev's affirmatively established goal of modernization signifies an attempt to overcome the oil curse Russian-style, which involves de-industrial-ization and decline of the sciences, and this discourse has contributed to further denigration of energy sec-tor hyper-development. By the end of Medvedev's presidency, the false start at executing the moderniza-tion proposition has compromised its rational content, so that Russia has come to depend more on oil and gas export revenues while the acknowledgement and even resentment of this dependency has spread from expert circles to the whole political class.[27]

It is quite uncertain whether the hydrocarbons would generate sufficient inflow of petro-dollars to finance the bloated social programs, but their di-

9

minishing political importance is quite certain. In the mid-2000s, the potential impact of the energy weapon was the subject of many alarmist assessments in the West, but at the start of the new decade, it has become clear for Moscow that opportunities for using energy towards political ends have all but disappeared.[28] Oil, which in fact generates most of the budget revenues, has zero political utility, and natural gas, which used to be the main focus of Western concerns, has become a product that requires a lot of political effort to market, particularly as a consequence of the massive increase of shale gas production in the United States.[29] Gazprom remains unable to open an export channel to China despite great many political commitments and has found itself under serious pressure to cut prices for Germany and other major consumers.[30] The much-anticipated opening of the *Nord Stream* pipeline across the Baltic Sea by the end of 2011 could improve reliability of Gazprom's deliveries, so it can hope to sell extra volumes to compensate for the interruption of supply from Libya, but the presumed geopolitical profile of this controversial pipeline is yet to be discovered.

The energy intrigues provide constant entertainment for professional Russia-watchers but they hide the trend of Russia's marginalization in the fast-moving economic globalization. Medvedev's attempt at breaking this trend by identifying directions where Russia could become a leader utilizing its scientific assets and cultivating high-tech innovations has been too feeble to make a difference, and the European Union (EU) initiative for promoting partnership for modernization has fallen perfectly flat.[31] The key condition for any progress in modernization is the inflow of foreign direct investments (FDI), but in reality Russia has experienced a colossal outflow of capital, estimated at

$134 billion in 2008, $56 billion in 2009, $35 billion in 2010, and continuing in 2011, despite Vladimir Putin's strict directive to secure the annual level of FDI at $60-70 billion.[32] Medvedev correctly characterized the Russian investment climate as very poor but has been pathetically helpless in inducing any changes, which would have inevitably involved curtailing interests of corrupt bureaucratic clans.[33]

Having accumulated foreign exchange and gold reserves of about $550 billion (as of September 2011), Russia could have been a major player in the global financial market, and Medvedev keeps insisting on the plan for organizing an international financial center in Moscow. Domestic confidence in Russian money-management is so low, however, that the ruble falls against the euro with every piece of sad news from the euro-zone.[34] Despite the relatively high and remarkably stable oil prices of 2011, investment funds prefer to move away from the Russian stock exchange, which keeps falling deeper than most world indexes during the current bumpy ride.[35] While the level of state debt is very low, the external corporate debt has grown again above $500 billion, most of which is made by state-owned corporations, so the costs of borrowing for covering the budget deficit could be even higher than its Better Business Bureau (BBB) credit rating indicates.[36] As the global economy is bracing for the next stage of the protracted crisis, Russia has nothing to contribute to addressing the central imbalances but is very vulnerable to negative external impacts.

GOING THROUGH THE MOTIONS IN INTERNATIONAL INSTITUTIONS

It is hard to find many bona fide liberal institution-alists among the Russian political elite, but Russia's foreign policy traditionally and persistently attaches great importance to demonstrating engagement in the works of various international institutions. Medvedev presents himself as a firm adherent to international law, and seeks to follow up on declarations with ac-tion, ranging from signing and ratifying the maritime border treaty with Norway to taking an assertive stance on the Kuril Islands dispute with Japan. He was also very eager to advance an ambitious proposal for a new legally binding treaty on European security that would have delegitimized war and provided the foundation for a new architecture."[37] What compro-mised this stance beyond all diplomatic white-wash-ing was the August 2008 war with Georgia, for which Moscow has never been able to build a convincing justification.[38] Medvedev was obliged to take respon-sibility for the consequences of this inglorious victory, but that has left him with little choice but to quietly abandon his grand Euro-architectural designs.[39]

The single most important position in all the in-stitutional miscellany is the permanent chair in the UN Security Council, so while Moscow periodically confirms its commitment to reforming this organ (par-ticularly to Germany and India), in fact, it is rather reluctant to invite new members to this hugely privi-leged club, and certainly does not want to hear about cancelling the veto right.[40] One of the major concerns in Russia's active engagement in the Security Coun-cil's proceedings (which contrasts with its rather low profile in most UN bodies) is upholding the centrality

12

of state sovereignty, so every interventionist measure, for instance in the spirit of the Responsibility to Protect doctrine, is scrutinized as an undesirable precedent.[41] For that matter, Moscow was extremely cautious about measuring every step in tightening the UN sanctions against Iran — and very upset by the enforcement of unilateral sanctions by the United States and the EU.[42] Medvedev had to defend the decision to let the UN Security Council pass Resolution 1973 on Libya against sharp criticism from Putin — and then was left complaining about NATO's abuse of this mandate for protecting civilians.[43] Russia wants to ensure that the UN remains the sole maker of international law, but this desire is clearly at cross-purposes with the preference for this unique organization to do as little as possible.

Another highly valued membership in an exclusive club is the hard-earned seat at the G-8 (United States, Japan, Germany, France, United Kingdom, Italy, Canada, and Russia), but this privilege has become diluted as the global crisis necessitated the shift of economic debates to the G-20 (Argentina, Australia, Brazil, Canada, China, France, Germany, India, Indonesia, Italy, Japan, Mexico, the Republic of Korea, Turkey, Russia, Saudi Arabia, South Africa, the United Kingdom, the United States, and the European Union). Seeking to ensure a special place as a connecting link, Moscow engages in transforming the odd grouping of Brazil, Russia, India, China, and South Africa (BRICS) into a real organization.[44] In fact, however, it cannot qualify as an emerging economy because it lacks economic dynamism and a growing population, so Russia is as much an odd man out in the company of China, India and Brazil, as it is among the seven industrial democracies. It is characteristic in this respect that Russia remains outside many key economic organizations: It has never been accepted into the G-7 (France, Germany, Italy, Japan, UK, the United States, and Canada) forum of finance ministers; despite being the major energy producer, it keeps its distance from the Organization of Petroleum Exporting Countries (OPEC) and does not take part in the International Energy Agency (IEA), while the Forum of gas producers has failed to grow into a real organization; its bid for joining the World Trade Organization (WTO) is still deadlocked and so membership in the Organization for Economic Cooperation and Development (OECD) is not in the cards.[45]

Russia is active in a great many overlapping regional organizations around its borders, from the Arctic Council to the Caspian "five" and to the Asia-Pacific Economic Cooperation (APEC), seeking to utilize the advantage of its unique geography. Political priority is formally set on cooperating with the post-Soviet neighbors, but the ambition to establish effective leadership in this natural sphere of influence has been derailed not only by reluctance to support this role with sufficient resources but also by arrogant and selfish political behavior. Every existing format from the broadest Commonwealth of Independent States (CIS), which functions mostly as a presidents' club, to the narrowest bilateral union state between Russia and Belarus, which has been bedeviled by quarrels with President Aleksandr Lukashenko, generates more problems than solutions.[46] Moscow is in a good position to exploit the post-Soviet autocrats' fears of domestic discontent escalating to revolution, but it is reluctant to commit itself to guaranteeing their regimes, so the Collective Security Treaty Organization (CSTO) remains a talk-shop despite recent declarations about making it into a shield against the threat of revolution.[47] Much expectation and concern has been focused on the potential of the Shanghai Cooperation Organization (SCO) to mature into an effective security provider, but Russia and China obviously have very different ideas about patronage over Central Asia.[48]

Russia, therefore, is prepared to engage with as many international institutions and regimes as possible only insofar as they aim at preserving the *status quo* (which most of them are built for) and securing for it a far more prominent global status than its economic weight or feeble soft power would justify. The mercantilist nature of its foreign policy, which conflates the interests of the corrupt authoritarian regime with national interests, determines the essentially unilateralist character of its external behavior.

CONCLUSIONS: THE BLUNDER OF INFLATED SELF-ASSESSMENT

In Russian political thinking, Russia's place in the world system is conceptualized not just as one of the great powers or poles in the multipolar world, but also as a unique position determined both by geography and by its development along a particular path. This model of a strong state directing economic and social development combines some features typical for Western democracies and some characteristics of the emerging powers, so that Russia could swing between various groups as it sees fit.[49] The problem with this ambitious vision is that the model does not work. Since the spasm of crisis in the autumn of 2008, Russia's petro-economy has generated insufficient revenues for sustaining the investments in strengthening the military might and the social cohesion, and the massive out-flow of capital proves that the class of super-rich has lost confidence in harvesting further profits.[50]

A major advantage of the Russian model is supposed to be political cohesion secured by the tightly centralized self-reproducing leadership, and it is exactly here that the crisis of Putinism has grown particularly malignant. The problem is not that the experimental construct of power-sharing between Putin and Medvedev is not organic to the hierarchic bureaucratic structure, but that the dominance of bureaucracy over business has resulted in unstoppable growth of corruption that has become the operational mode of this system of power rather than its side-effect.[51] The leadership will probably be reformatted after the tightly managed parliamentary and presidential elections, but that cannot restore the irreversibly diminished efficiency of a patently undemocratic political system.[52] Lacking soft power and discovering that its traditional hard power has become unusable or unreliable, Moscow finds itself not in the desired position of balancer but in the group of hopeless laggards, with no allies or friends and with the massive exposure to the phenomenon of China's growth.

This vulnerability should have been the central concern in Russia's foreign policy, but in fact, it is only a peripheral concern that leads to such seemingly odd moves as the deliberate escalation of the old quarrel with Japan over the South Kuril Islands.[53] The main focus of external activity is set on securing the regime's survival, and this obsession dictates an explicitly negative attitude towards any mass uprisings and revolutions, including those that have shaken the Arab world since the start of 2011.[54] This ideological stance that translates into readiness to stand by the Bashar al-

Assad regime in Syria no matter what crimes against own population it commits secures Moscow some moral leadership among the post-Soviet presidents-for-life and provides some foundation for a counter-revolutionary alliance with China.

This uncharacteristic departure from pragmatism, however, is not enough by far to compensate for the stalling reset with the United States and the deteriorating partnership with the EU, or to reverse the estrangement between Russia and its post-Soviet neighbors, or to erase China's growing contempt of Russia's self-made decline. It was Putin's resolute restoration of domestic order by the mid-2000s that underpinned the strengthening of Russia's international profile, and it is the deep degradation of Putinism that determines Russia's current marginalization in the chaotically changing international system while the ambitions of its national leader are still on the rise.

ENDNOTES - CHAPTER 1

1. Analysis of the trajectory of this crisis goes beyond the limited scope of this chapter, but its key parameters are examined in Maria Lipman and Nikolai Petrov, eds., *Russia in 2020: Scenarios for the Future*, Washington, DC: Carnegie Endowment for International Peace, 2011.

2. One sharp analysis of this concept is Vladislav Inozemtsev, "Dreams about a multi-polar world," *Nezavisimaya gazeta*, September 18, 2008; my examination is in Pavel Baev, "The Russian Federation: Striving for Multipolarity but Missing the Consequences," in Graeme Herd, ed., *Great Powers and Strategic Stability in the 21st Century*, London, UK: Routledge, 2010, pp. 117-136.

3. The transcript of the interview to Russian TV channels on August 31, 2008, in the English version of the presidential website, is available from *president.kremlin.ru/eng/speeches/2008/08/31/1850_type82912type82916_206003.shtml*.

4. An argument for rethinking the habitual articles of faith is presented in Fedor Lukyanov, "The West as a Problem," *Moskovskie novosti*, July 20, 2011; see also Nikolai Spassky, "The Island of Russia," *Russia in Global Affairs*, No. 2, April-June 2011.

5. Detailed analysis of Russia's nuclear posture can be found in several papers presented at the U.S. National Defense University and U.S. Army War College in 2010; see Steven Blank, ed., *Russian Nuclear Weapons: Past, Present, and Future*, Carlisle, PA: Strategic Studies Institute, U.S. Army War College, 2011. Yuri Solomonov, the chief designer of Russian solid-fueled intercontinental ballistic missiles (ICBMs), revealed the scope of the problems with funding and implementing the approved plans in an angry interview; see "State order for 2011 is already failed—it cannot be implemented," *Kommersant*, July 6, 2011.

6. Valuable updated information on the current developments is available in Pavel Podvig's blog, *Russian Strategic Nuclear Forces*, available from *russianforces.org/*.

7. Dmitri Rogozin, special envoy on missile defense matters, travels tirelessly around Europe selling the Russian position. See, for instance, Dmitri Rogozin, "Missile Defense: As friends or foes?" *New York Times*, June 7, 2011. In the growing body of Russian analysis, one noteworthy revisionist's view is found in Aleksandr Khramchihin, "Useless ABM—an artificially created reality," *Nezavisimoe voennoe obozrenie*, July 22, 2011.

8. On these failures, see "Russia's limited space," *Nezavisimoe voennoe obozrenie*, August 26, 2011. Acrimonious debates on the rationale of the air-space defense can be seen in Aleksandr Golts, "A package of incivility and slander," *Ezhednevny zhurnal*, August 5, 2011, available from *www.ej.ru/?a=note&id=11235*; Mikhail Khodarenok, "Elements of anti-missile heresy," *Voenno-promyshlennyi kuryer*, August 3, 2011, available from *vpk-news.ru/articles/7990*.

9. The content of Russia's nuclear policy is thoroughly examined in Aleksei Arbatov and Vladimir Dvorkin, *Nuclear Reset: Reduction and Proliferation of Weapons*, Moscow, Russia: POSSPEN, 2011.

10. One useful examination of this policy is Dmitri Trenin and Alexei Malashenko, "Iran: A View from Moscow," *Carnegie Report*, Moscow, Russia: Carnegie Center, October 2010. My recent analysis is in Pavel Baev, "Has Russia come to terms with Iran?" *PONARS Eurasia Memo* 141, Washington, DC: George Washington University, May 2011.

11. On the post-Fukushima aims of this activity, see Vadim Ponomarev, "No point in waiting," *Expert*, June 9, 2011; Vadim Dzaguto, "*Rosatom* is invited to the Emirates," *Kommersant*, August 16, 2011.

12. See Aleksei Arbatov, "Non-strategic nuclear weapons: Dilemmas and points of departure," *Nezavisimoe voennoe obozrenie*, May 20, 2011.

13. An attempt to escape from this trap is Sergei Karaganov, "To overcome deterrence," *Rossiiskaya gazeta*, April 6, 2011.

14. One noteworthy example of this thinking, which blends classical geopolitics with the clash of civilizations scheme and the Orthodox Christian dogmas, is the anonymous *Proekt Rossiya* (Project Russia) enterprise, which has published several books and expands its profile on the web; see *www.proektrussia.ru/*.

15. A more elegant presentation of this perspective, which compares Russia with a maverick planet that has escaped from the Western solar system, can be found in Dmitri Trenin, "Russia leaves the West," *Foreign Affairs*, Vol. 85, No. 4, July/August 2006, pp. 87-96.

16. A sample of the NATO-damning analysis is Aleksandr Bartosh, "US + NATO: Power Tandem of Globalization," *Nezavisimoe voennoe obozrenie*, March 11, 2011.

17. See Igor Yurgens, "Military cooperation: Breakthrough in Russia-NATO relations," *Vedomosti*, September 20, 2010.

18. A concise summary of this perspective is found in Sergei Karaganov, "Russia is in luck," *Rossiiskaya gazeta*, March 7, 2011.

19. See Fedor Lukyanov, "Colonial precedent," *Gazeta.ru*, August 28, 2011, available from *www.gazeta.ru/column/lukyanov/3744173.shtml*.

20. This assessment is fairly close to some U.S. analyses, see, for instance, Stephen Fidler and Alistair Macdonald, "European retreat on defense spending," *Wall Street Journal*, August 24, 2011.

21. An informed and positive assessment of the initial stage of the reform can be found in Vitaly Shlykov, "The secrets of Serdyukov's blitzkrieg," *Russia in Global Affairs*, January/March 2010, pp. 29-48. Further stages are examined in M.S. Barabanov, ed., *Novaya Armiya Rossii (Russia's New Army)*, Moscow, Russia: AST, 2010; Aleksei Arbatov and Vladimir Dvorkin, "Russian New Military Reform," *Carnegie Paper*, Moscow, Russia: June 2011. My less upbeat analysis can be found in Pavel K. Baev, "Military reform against heavy odds," in Anders Åslund, Sergei Guryev, and Andrew Kuchins, eds., *Russia after the Global Economic Crisis*, Washington, DC: Peterson Institute for International Economics, 2010, pp. 169-186.

22. Medvedev gives Serdyukov support in squeezing the suppliers, but the state corporations have allies in Putin's cabinet; see Ivan Safronov, "President controls the state defense order," *Kommersant*, July 13, 2011; Viktor Myasnikov, "State-defense-failure: price war, corruption, and arms-twisting," *Nezavisimoe voennoe obozrenie*, July 22, 2011.

23. On the purchase of a complete training center from *Rheinmetall*, see Vlad Socor, "Made in Germany for Russia's army," *Eurasia Daily Monitor*, February 14, 2011.

24. My most recent analysis of this departure from geopolitics is in Pavel Baev, "Russia's Ambivalent Arctic Policy: Asserting Sovereignty and Advancing Cooperation," paper presented at the Kingston Conference on International Security, June 13-15, 2011.

25. See on that Aleksei Malashenko, "What the North Caucasus Means to Russia," *Russie.Nei.Visions*, Vol. 61, Paris, France: *Institut français des relations internationales* (IFRI), July 2011.

26. One authoritative source on that is Marshall I. Goldman, *Petrostate: Putin, Power and the New Russia*, Oxford, UK: Oxford University Press, 2008. I have examined the energy-political ambitions in Pavel Baev, *Russian Energy Policy and Military Power*, London, UK: Routledge, 2008.

27. See Vladimir Milov, "Russian Economy in Limbo," *Pro et Contra*, Vol. 15, No. 1-2, January-April 2011, available from *http://russia-2020.org/2010/07/13/russian-economy-in-limbo/*; Sergei Guriev, "Oil cannot save us," *Forbes* (Russian Ed.), January 20, 2011, available from *www.forbes.ru/ekonomika-column/finansy/62301-neft-uzhe-ne-spasaet*.

28. The popular propositions like, "It is on this front, of energy blackmail, that Russia has been most active," were problematic to start with, and now need further re-evaluation. See Edward Lucas, *The New Cold War: Putin's Russia and the Threat to the West*, New York: Palgrave Macmillan, 2009, p. xix.

29. The course of the shale gas revolution is examined in the *World Energy Outlook 2009*, Paris, France: IEA, 2009; see particularly pp. 400-415. One sharp view is Holman W. Jenkins, Jr., "Shale Gas and Putin Puzzle," *Wall Street Journal*, June 22, 2011. Meeting with the Valdai club in November 2011, Putin expressed strong views on this issue; see Clifford Gaddy and Fiona Hill, "Putin's Next Move in Russia," *CUSE Comments*, December 12, 2011, available from *www.brookings.edu/interviews/2011/1212_putin_gaddy_hill.aspx*.

30. On the deadlocked bargaining with China, see Sergei Kulikov, "Gazprom is surrounded by opponents of expensive gas," *Nezavisimaya gazeta*, August 18, 2011; on the issues with Germany, see Konstantin Simonov, "How much gas does Germany need?" *Expert*, July 26, 2011.

31. An insightful view on that is Arkady Moshes, "Europe is tired of Russia," *Gazeta.ru*, June 10, 2011, available from *gazeta.ru/comments/2011/06/10_x_3658765.shtml*.

32. See Sergei Minaev, "The depth of powerful outflow," *Kommersant-Vlast*, June 20, 2011; on Putin's directive, see Igor Naumov, "Putin wants to bring back investors," *Nezavisimaya gazeta*, March 28, 2011.

33. See Catherine Belton and Charles Clover, "Medvedev expected to target capital flight," *Financial times*, May 5, 2011.

34. See Aleksandr Morozov, "Ruble will lose," *Forbes* (Russian Ed.), August 29, 2011, available from *http://www.forbes.ru/lichnye-dengi-column/valyuty/72753-rubl-proigraet*.

35. See Anton Verzhbitsky, "Foreigners take money out of Russia en masse," *RBC Daily*, August 29, 2011.

36. On the looming budget issues, see Aleksei Mihailov, "Budget of war and police," *Gazeta.ru*, July 25, 2011, available from *www.gazeta.ru/column/mikhailov/3707805.shtml*; on Putin's irritation over the too low credit rating, see "Russia and US find common foe in S&P," *Moscow Times*, August 10, 2011.

37. One attempt to sell this proposal is Dmitri Danilov, "The European Security Treaty within the EU-US-NATO Triangle," *Security Index*, Vol. 16, No. 4, Fall 2010, pp. 61-72.

38. Careful examination of this self-acquitting can be found in Roy Allison, "The Russian case for military intervention in Georgia: International law, norms and political calculation," *European Security*, Vol. 18, No. 2, June 2009, pp. 173-200.

39. My short comment on this can be found in Pavel Baev, "Medvedev reflects on the Georgian war and on himself," *Eurasia Daily Monitor*, August 8, 2011.

40. It is hard to find anything on Russia's contribution on the very useful website of the Center for UN Reform, which has a special page for the Security Council reform; see *www.center forunreform.org/node/23*.

41. See Fedor Lukyanov, "Aria of the off-stage choir," *Gazeta.ru*, June 23, 2011, available from *gazeta.ru/column/lukyanov/3672037.shtml*.

42. One isolated voice of reason is Dmitri Trenin, "Russia, uranium and Iran," *InoSMI.ru*, June 10, 2010, available from *inosmi.ru/op_ed/20100611/160522302.html*.

43. See Aleksandr Aksenenok, "Russian diplomacy in the Libyan crisis," *Moskovskie novosti*, July 21, 2011; Nikolai Zlobin, "Why Russia is not Libya," *Vedomosti*, March 28, 2011.

44. On the weakness of this grouping, see Fedor Lukyanov, "BRICS into pebbles," *Gazeta.ru*, June 2, 2011, available from *gazeta.ru/column/lukyanov/3636225.shtml*; the idea to invite Turkey is found in Dmitri Trenin, "Ankara as a geopolitical partner for Moscow," *InoSMI.ru*, April 29, 2011, available from *inosmi.ru/op_ed/20110429/168896495.html*.

45. On the latter problem, see Aleksei Portansky, "Russia's accession to the WTO: External implications," *Russia in Global Affairs*, No. 2, April/June 2011, available from *eng.globalaffairs.ru/number/Russias-Accession-to-the-WTO-External-Implications-15239*.

46. One of the most thoughtful analysts of political processes in this space was Dmitri Furman; see, for instance, his lecture "From the Russian Empire to the Failure of the CIS," *Polit.ru*, October 5, 2005, available from *www.polit.ru/article/2005/10/05/furman/*.

47. On the latest summit of this quasi-alliance, see Aleksandr Gabuev, "CSTO tries to become a bloc," *Kommersant*, August 13, 2011; Viktor Litovkin, "CSTO is turned against the color revolutions," *Nezavisimoe voennoe obozrenie*, September 9, 2011; informed analysis is Roger McDermott, "CSTO moves into the information age," *RFE/RL Commentary*, September 4 2011, available from *www.rferl.org/content/commentary_csto_moves_into_information_age/24317363.html*.

48. On the tensions in this smoothly-run body, see Vladimir Skosyrev, "Russian influence in Central Asia is diminishing," *Nezavisimaya gazeta*, April 27, 2011; Fedor Lukyanov, "SCO as a global mirror," *Gazeta.ru*, June 16, 2011, available from *gazeta.ru/column/lukyanov/3663441.shtml*.

49. For dualism, see Evgeny Gontmaher, "Between catching-up and innovative modernization," *Vedomosti*, August 31, 2011.

50. On the drivers for the capital flight, see Sergei Shelin, "Money chose freedom," *Gazeta.ru*, May 25, 2011, available from *www.gazeta.ru/column/shelin/3628261.shtml*.

51. Literature on corruption in Russia is vast, but a value of evidence is available at the blog of Aleksei Navalny, available from *navalny.ru/*.

52. The crisis of leadership is diagnosed even by the professional courtiers; see for instance, Gleb Pavlovsky, "Tandem has turned into a thrombus in the Russian state," *Novaya gazeta*, August 17, 2011.

53. My take can be found in Pavel Baev, "Moscow learns to play by Asia-Pacific rules," *Eurasia Daily Monitor*, February 14, 2011.

54. See Vitaly Naumkin, "From the bottom to the top and back," *Russia in Global Affairs*, No. 4, July/August 2011, available from *www.globalaffairs.ru/number/Snizu-vverkh-i-obratno-15277*.

CHAPTER 2

THE SACRED MONSTER:
RUSSIA AS A FOREIGN POLICY ACTOR

Stephen J. Blank

INTRODUCTION

Writing in 2002, Russia's Foreign Minister, Igor Ivanov, proclaimed that the Russian Federation was qualitatively different from all of its Russian predecessors. According to Ivanov, Russia differed from them in its nature of government, territorial boundaries, the geopolitical environment it faced, and in its capabilities and power. Therefore, it "needed to develop a new way of looking at its foreign policy goals and priorities." Ivanov further argued that Russia did not and implicitly does not see itself as heir to the Soviet policy in pursuing a foreign policy dictated by the requirements of an international class war.[1] Therefore, according to Ivanov, Moscow no longer pursues a policy based on a fixed idea of a particular enemy or adversary and has renounced all the trappings of Leninism, including an ideological approach to foreign policy. Since then, according to Ivanov and many other commentators, Russia has instead struggled, finally with success in recent years, to conduct a foreign policy based solely on the pursuit of national interests.

But is this the whole story? While Russia certainly no longer pursues a "class-based" foreign policy based on Marxism-Leninism; and certainly manifests a horror of revolution abroad today, is Russian foreign policy under Vladimir Putin and his successor, Dmitry Medvedev, really a qualitatively new foreign policy, or are there significant elements of enduring Russian approaches to foreign policy that developed during the Tsarist and Soviet periods of Russian history? Is there no ideological component to Russian foreign policy and only the strict pursuit of national interests, obviously conceived of in a manner resembling the 19th century fashion? Can Russia, or any other state for that matter, escape history and start anew even if we allow for a new environment and new (and reduced) capabilities for exercising power? Or is it, in fact, the case, as certainly appears to be developing in Russia's domestic politics and maybe its foreign policy, that Russia is *to some considerable extent* still enmeshed in its past history? Is it the case, in contrast to Ivanov's argument, that, as the contemporary Russian novelist Vladimir Sorokin says, "Our future is becoming our past"?[2] In that case, would not Russian foreign policy under Putin reflect, as well, the siren call and abiding forces of Russian history?

INNOVATION AND CONTINUITY

Without denying substantial and ongoing change (which also visibly occurred under the Soviet system), this work argues that Russian policy, despite undoubted innovations, is less innovative than Ivanov claimed. We argue here that much of the tone and content of Russian foreign policy represents an outward projection of its autocratic domestic political system and that system's attendant mentality. Indeed, the leaders of this system consciously and frequently invoke Russian history as a justification for its continuation in power.[3] Therefore this continuity allows us to judge Moscow's foreign policy from within a framework of Russia's historical development. We use this term autocratic because it is obvious to us and to several other writers that today's Russian state bears many defining characteristics that resemble in considerable degree, if not always totally, Tsarist and Soviet precedents. Just as both the Tsarist system, as it evolved over time, and the Soviet system exemplified the patrimonial Russian state; so too does the current system represent a patrimonial autocratic system as defined below. That state is characterized by personified power, currently in the form of the President or even the tandem of Putin and Medvedev and state ownership of property at the expense of legally enshrined property rights. It also manifests itself in the recurrence of a modified version of the old service state and the feudal relationship of patron and client networks or the phenomenon of *nul home sans seigneur* (no man without a lord) that typified feudalism. Indeed, many scholars have recognized this linkage between what we might call the domestic constitution and foreign policy.[4] For example, Alexei Arbatov states that:

> This interdependence between the regime's nature at home and its projection abroad explains why those trying now to rehabilitate Stalinism and appeal for a return to this or that form of authoritarian regime always link it to a revival of some form of Russian (or Soviet) empire and permanent confrontation with the West.[5]

The announced transfer of power in September 2011 whereby Premier Putin and President Medvedev announced that they would exchange positions in 2012 indicates that for the ruling elite, the state is conceived of, indeed, as nothing more than Putin's personal property, or to use the old Russian term for patrimony (*Votchina*), upon which he can act as he pleases. This patrimonial attitude confirms the genetic resemblance to Tsarist and Soviet models of the state. This recent ministerial or presidential leapfrog between Medvedev and Putin, to use the late Tsarist term, validates our use of the concept of patrimonialism because it so vividly demonstrates this concept's continuing practice, along with its subordinate manifestations of an enduring contempt for law and for the Russian people. It also is arguably a vote for the entropy of the system as occurred under Leonid Brezhnev and arguably a guarantee that sooner or later, though we cannot say when, why, or how this will occur, a violent crisis will shake the system. Indeed, Putin's spokesman recently contended that "For us, Brezhnev is not a minus sign but rather a positive sign."[6]

This patrimonial state formation is a recurrent phenomenon in Russian history. Therefore, we employ here a historically-based explanation of contemporary Russia's foreign policy continuity with its forbears. While this approach is certainly not the last or even necessarily the first word in analyzing contemporary Russian policy, it does represent an under-represented view or word that must nevertheless be spoken. Certainly the evidence of congruence with past governmental systems is there for any observer to find. For example, as it developed into the 19th and 20th century, the autocracy spawned a vast but incoherent bureaucracy that made it ever more difficult for the Tsar or for policymakers to control policy, not least foreign policy. Thus Heinrich Vogel observed that:

> It is becoming more and more clearly evident that President Putin can place only limited trust in the officials of the partially reformed public institutions. The Kremlin is granted obsequious obedience in suppressing undesirable political activities, and the resulting

political correctness engenders lip service to a strong state; but the most immediate loyalty is to each local authority.[7]

Today's Russian press is filled with repeated instances of both Medvedev's and Putin's repeated frustration and anger over the systematic inability to implement state policies or willful disobedience by bureaucrats, much as was the case in the Tsarist and Soviet past.

Due to the failure to reform, today there is neither a lawful or specifically legislated overall policy process for resolving critical foreign or defense policies nor a specific institution legally ordained with regular and general oversight and leadership of national security policy. The long lasting struggle between the General Staff and the Ministry of Defense as well as the fluctuating status of the Security Council graphically testify to this fact, and the consequences of this absence emerged clearly in both the descent into Pristina and the second Chechen war, both in 1999, and has now morphed into the entire North Caucasus, two episodes that show how easily the unchecked rashness of the General Staff, supported by the regime, could entrap Russia either in big or in endless wars, if not both[8]

Thus Russia still lacks a reliable and consistent or stable mechanism for either making or conducting defense policy. Those who claim otherwise, like former Defense Minister Sergei Ivanov as former Secretary of the Security Council, must hide or distort the truth. Like Tsarist statesmen, they pretend that a regular, law-governed bureaucratic process or system is occurring in defense policymaking and that a regularly functioning institution or institutions are currently making or coordinating policy[9] However, as they well know, the reality is exactly the opposite of a regularly functioning system. Indeed, every reliable account of how the system actually operates points to a system of unending and often vicious bureaucratic struggle. Accordingly, major policy questions, and not just on defense policy, are always subject to obstruction by interested bureaucracies and to lack of coordinated follow through. Alternatively major policy initiatives are launched behind the government's back so to speak, denoting a continuing failure to devise even what Soviet scholars called a rule of law government (Pravovoye Gosudarstvo). This disorganization typified the late Tsarist regime's approach to policymaking, and students of Soviet history know full well how much bureaucratic infighting and lack of coordination occurred there. In this respect, contemporary Russian national security policy (and probably other realms of policymaking as well) are eerily reminiscent of late Tsarist Russia when Baron A. P. Izvol'skii, about to be named Foreign Minister, told the Quai D'Orsay that:

> 'Despotism' always bore the same fruits — 'incoherence if not contradiction in the conduct of affairs which are treated simultaneously by various departments which ignore each other — and which obtain from the supreme leader detailed decisions which are irreconcilable in fact: the Russo-Japanese War came from that."[10]

This failure to achieve political reform has therefore precluded genuine military reform and civilian control of the multiple armed forces. This gap in control over the structures of force (Silovye Struktury) impedes democratization, because it leaves control of the military outside of the normally functioning democratic channels of control, and undermines Russia's ability to maximize its security position in international affairs because Russian policy is ad hoc, unpredictable, and subject to no regularized institutions of policy control. It also impedes Russia's ability to defend itself against real threats like the jihadi insurgency in the North Caucasus.

For example, President Putin's proposals in 2000 for a missile defense initiative involving Europe to counter the U.S. missile defense program were worked out without consultation or participation by either the Ministry of Defense or Foreign Affairs.[11] Not surprisingly, there were public expressions of dissent by powerful military figures like the Commander in Chief (CINC) of the Strategic Nuclear forces, General Vladimir Yakovlev, that outside observers could not reconcile with Putin's statements and which left everyone confused as to what the policy really was.[12] Former Finance Minister Alexei Kudrin's September 2011 outburst against excessive defense spending cited below suggests that this phenomenon of struggle and lack of control over the instruments of force continues, even if it is generally carefully hidden behind the Kremlin's walls.

FOREIGN AND DEFENSE POLICY CONTINUITY

Today Arbatov, among many, laments the absence of coherent policymaking mechanisms or institutions, Parliament's nullity as a counterweight to the executive, and the predominance of informal relationships at the top that break down any attempt at orderly policymaking, even within the executive.[13] Izvol'skii and his colleagues would undoubtedly find themselves at home in today's Russia; so would post-Stalin Soviet bureaucrats, if not their predecessors. Thus Andrei

Ryabov writes that, "Freedom and ownership rights gave not been given an institutional framework, nor has there been a return to the numerous rules that the old system had for regulating the elite's recruitment and transfer of power." Moreover, power remains personified, not regulated by law. Putin's primacy as Premier, constitutionally the No. 2 position in the government after 2008 and the recent exchange of positions with Medvedev demonstrate this.[14] Indeed, discerning analysts see in Putin's regime a kind of reversion to aspects of Stalinist personnel practice or policy, whereby police or security services cadre play the role of both the party and the security services under Joseph Stalin. Thus already in 2004, Nikolai Petrov wrote that:

> The old system of appointment and staff rotation has been reduplicated. Establishing an infrastructure of secret services the local police do not control, the federal center regained the previously lost leverage with the regions. Shifting representation in law enforcement agencies, the president ended up with a "security horizontal" at his service. Along with the executive verticals, it forms a kind of carcass holding the state together. To a certain extent, the authorities have reduplicated the Stalin system when control over regional elites was maintained through (and with encouragement of) a confrontation between party organizations and security structures. In conflicts like that, the federal center is always well informed on everything. These days, we have a conflict between security structures and regional elites. State officials feel themselves under observation and abstain from what they were free to do only recently.[15]

More recently, Gregory Carleton has written that:

> To frame contemporary culture without reference to the Soviet legacy would seem irresponsible — just as this article cannot avoid. Moreover, current realities give credence to this logic. The centralization of power by United Russia, the consequent emergence of an identifiable single party line, the state's key control of key sectors of the economy, and the suppression of independent media — all, inter alia, recall Soviet practice and policies. Additional corroboration of this impression comes from the conscious resurrection of Soviet symbols, such as the national anthem and the flood of Stalinist hagiography, particularly as popular history, with some of it more grandiose and fictitious than what circulated in his lifetime.[16]

In other words, we see multiple signs of regression to past Soviet and Tsarist practices. Moreover, these reversions go well beyond the examples cited here to encompass much, if not all, of Russia's socio-economic-political and even cultural life. Therefore contemporary observers do not hesitate to describe the bureaucracy as patrimonial.[17]

To the degree that the Russian elite, beginning with President Boris Yeltsin (1991-99), consciously opted to rebuild an autocratic system of power in the traditional sense, it also adopted both the trappings and substance of many historical policies that have characterized Russia over the years. Among these traditional manifestations of Russian autocratic thinking and policy are an obsession with Russia's uniqueness or specificity (Samobytnost' or Spetsifichnost' in Russian), its refusal to account to anyone at home or abroad for its actions (itself a projection outward of autocratic power) to other governments, and the neo-imperial concept of the state that is explainable not only in terms of material interest, but also in Russia's obsession with status and in the relentless quest for an exclusive sphere of influence in the former Soviet Union at the expense of the sovereignty of the new states there. Lastly, there are a series of geopolitical continuities with past regimes, the presupposition that Russia is threatened by enemies everywhere and thus must have a free hand in its policies and not be subordinate to anyone (itself linked with the autocratic impulse), the enduring obsession with the United States as the main enemy and also most desired partner, and the constant effort to prevent any kind of European integration or at least to freeze it in its tracks.

To be sure, no state can simply abandon its history without incurring serious, diverse, and long-term costs. Indeed, the fundamental changes in Russia since 1991 are incontestable. This goes beyond the end of Marxism-Leninism, support for socialists and revolutionaries abroad, a planned economy, and at least until now, the excessive militarization of the economy. Likewise, the priority placed on economic instruments in foreign and domestic policy and Russia's unprecedented wealth represent fundamental changes. But even here, in this most innovative realm of Putin's foreign and defense policy, we find traditional elements holding their ground, so to speak. Moreover, we find some distinctly disquieting signs of a pervasive moral nihilism that has accompanied and been both cause and outcome of the endemic corruption and unbridled criminality of the Russian political system, one that Medvedev described as legal nihilism. Logically, it should not surprise observers that the progression from legal nihilism and the ongoing failure to confront honestly the Soviet historical record has contributed greatly to this pervasive moral nihilism.

As Dmitri Trenin recently observed, much elite thinking sees international politics as simply a struggle for power between competitive states where values and their invocation merely cloaks hard power designs.[18] Essentially, this is a bastardized version of Otto Bismarck's realism that harks back to conservative German thought in the 19th and 20th centuries as embodied by people like Friedrich Nietszche, Carl Schmitt, etc.[19] Ironically, as is the case with so much Russian social theory after 1800, there is much that is originally German more than intrinsically Russian in it, except possibly for its intransigent absolutism and extreme nihilism that there is nothing beyond this struggle for power in international relations. Thus Russia, like China, is a pillar of the "high church of realism" in international affairs. Its realism, as described by Trenin and discussed below, is of a particularly atavistic and even nihilistic kind that believes in nothing but power.[20] Therefore, its thinking and behavior antedate the theories of realism in world politics that appeared after World War II and are a throwback to 19th century Realpolitik of a particularly brutal kind.

Trenin incisively captures the worldview of the elite and the practical consequences that flow from it.

- The world is primarily one of struggle of all against all, of fierce competition for markets and resources. Cooperation emerges not out of good will but competition, whose point is to determine the conditions on which future cooperation may be possible.
- Economics are paramount, and business and money are both driving forces and the prize. There is no room for emotions in this competition or for values.

- Consequently, Western values that are so highly prized there are merely covers, cloaks for a reality every bit as harsh and no different from that in Russia where money and power are king. Democracy promotion is merely a tool for promoting U.S. interests.
- Russia is strategically alone, but only needs itself as it is self-sufficient. Other major powers are its rivals and smaller powers the objects and purpose of these struggles.
- Russia's key comparative advantages, at least for the foreseeable future, are oil and gas and its nuclear weapons, the most important guarantors of its security.

The practical consequences of this cynical *Weltanschauung* are:
- Realpolitik is the only reliable policy.
- Maintaining the status of a great power under autocratic rule is the precondition for Russia's survival and progress as a great power, which means that smaller states orbit around its sun. Otherwise, Russia will be torn apart.
- Everyone is a potential competitor or partner at least for a time but because nobody and nothing can be trusted and they will cheat at the first instance (as will Russia), legally binding contracts or agreements are necessary (but nothing guarantees that Russia will stay bound, because the others are no better and only interest guides Russia).
- Foreign policy is guided only by the national interest, which in Russia means the interest of the ruling corporation.

- Interests, not illusory ideology or values, represent the real substance of foreign policy. Pragmatism consists of managing differing and opposing interests.
- Patriotism is only important for mobilizing the public and creating a solid base for a pragmatic foreign policy.
- Public opinion is only the result of external manipulation by interested parties and experts. The manipulation of images that are created and destroyed on demand trumps any concept of reputation.
- Foreign policy relationships must be maintained with everyone but without any ideological or value-grounded expectations.
- The aim of Russian foreign policy is the creation or formation of a Russian center of power as one constitutive element of the emerging world order, a global oligarchy of five or six key players. Only when American hegemonism passes into history, which Moscow believes is happening, can there be a basis for genuine partnership with America.

As a result, we have a foreign policy elite that is utterly cynical, manipulative, exceptionally venal, and obsessed with power, wealth, and status. While its utter cynicism may go beyond even the Soviet system, the pervasive moral nihilism that is so strong a Soviet legacy is deeply visible here, as is the late 19th century origin of such views. It is narrow-minded, less informed about the world than its predecessors, amoral, and not interested in bettering the life of the people or in overcoming the traditional gap between state and society. It has contempt for the people instead, and national interest is often a cloak for personal or sectoral interests. As it has no strategy other than narrow self-interest, its policies are reactive and essentially negative threats to obstruct if Russia is not respected. Those members of the elite who are familiar with the outside world, like all nouveaux riches, think they know the price of everyone and everything, and that they know it all, when in fact much of what they know is essentially conspiracies to gain power and wealth among elites who are as corrupt, self-seeking, and venal as they are. They are at once driven by a paradoxical combination familiar to students of Russian history and culture of an inferiority complex and an ingrained sense of superiority and overcompensation. Thus their behavior is often boorish, uninformed, and characterized by a resort to crude threats and intimidation, which, after all, is the way they get things done at home.[21]

If one compares this with the behavior of gangsters who are obsessed with respect and status as well as power and wealth and possess a similarly cynical world view and amorality regarding the means of obtaining these goals, it becomes clear why so many observers rightly characterize Russia as a "mafia state." After all, the Mafia and the current state are essentially medieval formations that have adapted but retain their core essence. Moreover, as described below the regime has, in its foreign policy, aligned itself with organized crime abroad as an instrument of state policy.

At the same time, Putin's and his team's realization of the primacy of the need to develop a modern economy in Russia and use economic power as the foundation of Russia's global standing marks a significant innovation in Russia's history. Only after economic stability was achieved do we now see significant increases in defense spending, a pattern also seen in the 1930s. But the ultimate goal of advancing the great power standing and capacity of the state is entirely traditional in nature, as is the belief that the state must lead this process by itself without reference to indigenous self-standing social networks.[22] Equally traditional is the fact of the state's penchant for militarism. Historians repeatedly mocked the paradomania for endless strict military parades of Tsars Paul, Alexander I, and Nicholas I, and the legacy of state militarism that the Tsars as a whole fostered continues to inhibit defense reform in Russia.[23]

Similarly, critics of the regime, notably former economics officials, like Aleksei Kudrin (Finance Minister 2000-11) and Andrei Illarionov (President Putin's economic advisor), have both publicly criticized the regime's excessive defense spending and tendency to think in terms of war. In September 2011, Kudrin announced that he would not serve under the forthcoming Prime Minister Medvedev (currently President Medvedev) and specifically attacked excessive defense spending.[24] Illarionov has observed that:

> Since its outset, the Siloviki regime has been aggressive. At first it focused on actively destroying centers of independent political, civil, and economic life within Russia. Upon achieving those goals, the regime's aggressive behavior turned outward beyond Russia's borders. At least since the assassination of the former Chechen President Zelimkhan Yandarbiyev in Doha, Qatar on 14 February 2004, aggressive behavior by SI [Siloviki-men of the structures of force-author] in the international arena has become the rule rather than the exception. Over the last five years the regime has waged ten different "wars" (most of them involving propaganda, intelligence operations, and economic coercion rather than open military force)

against neighbors and other foreign nations. The most recent targets have included Ukraine (subjected to a "second gas war" in early 2009), The United States (subjected to a years-long campaign to rouse anti-American sentiment), and, most notoriously, Georgia (actually bombed and invaded in 2008). In addition to their internal psychological need to wage aggressive wars, a rational motive is also driving the Siloviki to resort to conflict. War furnishes the best opportunities to distract domestic public opinion and destroy the remnants of the political and intellectual opposition within Russia itself. An undemocratic regime worried about the prospect of domestic economic social and political crises — such as those that now haunt Russia amid recession and falling oil prices — is likely to be pondering further acts of aggression. The note I end on, therefore, is a gloomy one: To me the probability that Siloviki Incorporated well be launching new wars seems alarmingly high.[25]

There can be no doubt that many of the methods used by Moscow reek of traditional coercive Russian socio-political interactions, not to mention outright criminality.

Given Kudrin's well-founded misgivings about the direction of policy, it is too soon to tell if this priority of economics represents a long-term and stable trend or one that could or will give way, as may increasingly be possible, to renewed emphasis on overt military great power rivalry. Certainly the statist and dirigiste notion of economic development that now prevails in Moscow augurs badly for democracy or for optimal economic growth but strongly for the perpetuation of the Muscovite paradigm with its emphasis on de-fense. That trend is highly likely to lead logically to an increase in military rivalry and political tensions with other major powers, as has historically been the case. The substantial rise in defense spending and increasingly military cast of the rivalry with America is a warning sign in this regard. For if the end result of Putinism is a renewed militarization, then the innovative aspects of his legacy will diminish while the assertion of traditional practices and policies will have triumphed. Indeed, as of early 2012, we see disturbing signs in this regard.[26]

Nonetheless, as Putin and his team have recognized, Russia's ability to compete in world politics or to maintain its sovereign and independent freedom of action in their terms, crucially depends upon its ability to build and sustain a vibrant technologically advanced economy. Only on this basis can it compete in world politics while simultaneously building a military capable of defending the national interest. Although Russia is currently undertaking a significant, if not major, military buildup to last through 2020 and its emphasis upon the military arm is growing (not least due to domestic reasons connected with the succession to Putin in 2008), Putin's overall policies have hitherto been distinguished by an understanding of the priority of the economic instrument of statecraft over the military one. This also relates to the primacy of a perception of domestic rather than foreign threats in actual policy, as for example in the share of the national security budget allocated to the armed forces and to those agencies primarily responsible for domestic security like the Ministry of Interior.[27]

This understanding of the priority of economic reconstruction and of the economic instrument in foreign policy is also apparent in Russian foreign policies towards the Commonwealth of Independent States (CIS), in the extensive dialogue with the European Union (EU), and in its use of the energy weapon in Europe and Asia. Even the primary purpose of arms sales has arguably been, until about 2005 if not later, the acquisition of revenue that would allow the Russian defense industry to recover until it can provide for the domestic rearmament of the Russian military. Indeed, as Foreign Minister Sergei Lavrov has acknowledged, it is "the energy weapon" that has allowed Russia to gain independence in foreign policy vis-à-vis its numerous interlocutors.[28] On a daily basis, energy exports, particularly of natural gas, are Russia's principal foreign policy instrument. Arguably, no major power has ever before staked its great power standing and identity so nakedly on this cash crop to the extent that Russia has. This policy, or more precisely grand strategy, of employing energy as an all-purpose instrument of national strategy in several different regions was canonized in Russia's 2003 energy strategy that openly postulated the connection between Russia's ability to export large energy volumes, mainly to Europe but subsequently as well to East Asia, and its great power standing.[29]

That energy strategy, subsequent statements by President Putin and other leading officials confirm the importance of energy to Russia's foreign policy, and that energy policy's purpose is to promote Russia's return to great power status in Eurasia.[30] Indeed, as Roman Kupchinsky pointed out, Moscow in 2009 formally admitted in its 2009 national security concept that:

> The change from bloc confrontation to the principles of multi-vector diplomacy and the [natural] resources potential of Russia, along with the pragmatic policies of using them has expanded the possibilities of the Russian Federation to strengthen its influence on the world arena. In other words, Russia's energy resourc-

es were once again officially acknowledged to be tools of Russian foreign policy, or as some believe, a lever for blackmail. There was apparently no further reason for denying the obvious, and the authors of the [2009] security doctrine decided to lay out Russia's cards on the table.[31]

Although there is a conscious effort to augment Russia's real capabilities for projecting military power into the borderlands, that hardly equates to the use of that power to enforce compliance with its wishes. Russia uses energy exports as a multipurpose security instrument, much like a Swiss Army knife that cuts in all directions.[32]

However, at the same time, we have more recently seen a careful and consistent effort to rebuild Russian military capability and its capacity for projecting effective power throughout the CIS, most notably in Central Asia. Thus Russia has been selling to Central Asian states Russian weapons at subsidized prices, providing training, buying up former Soviet defense industrial facilities on their territories in exchange for debts, building up its military bases in Kyrgyzstan, Tajikistan, and potentially Uzbekistan (in case there is an emergency, Russia has the legal right to use the air base at Navoi[33]), building an expanded Caspian Flotilla, augmenting military capabilities for rapid power projection into Central Asia, constructing integrated military alliances with Central Asian states through the Collective Security Treaty Organization (CSTO) and a projected Caspian naval force (CASFOR), and by dropping not so subtle hints that the Shanghai Cooperation Organization (SCO) should become either or both a military alliance and / or an energy club.[34]

In so doing, Russia has several objectives. First, Russia seeks to create a network of defense and defense industrial relationships spanning both Central and East Asia. Towards this end, it has either begun to conduct or announced a series of exercises to unite its own forces with those of Central Asian allies in the SCO, China, and India, e.g., the August 2005 naval exercises with Kazakhstan and other states in the Caspian. Operation Tsentr' exercises in September 2011, and annual exercises among the SCO members, including bilateral exercises with China after 2005, exemplify this policy. Second, Russia seeks to transform the SCO into a true strategic and military alliance whereas China has openly advocated that it concentrate on trade and economics. Third, Russia's force development and base seeking campaigns aim to provide its forces in Central Asia with integrated ground, air, and naval (Caspian Sea Flotilla) forces. The recent Russian moves to gain new bases in Uzbekistan, Kyrgyzstan, and Tajikistan also clearly aim at providing secure lodgments for expanding air and ground forces, especially as its own domestic defense reforms aim at generating a real, as opposed to notional, capability for moving forces rapidly to hot spots, a theme that has been rehearsed frequently in its exercises since 2004.[35]

Thus careful analysis of Putin's policies suggests that we should not be overly hasty in concluding that there is a long-term depreciation of the military instrument in Russian policy. Putin has had to grapple with years of neglect and bad policy and has in his own way contributed to the abiding dilemmas of Russian defense reconstruction.[36] The new arms buildup also suggests a recurrence or at least an attempt to foster the recurrence of what the Russian historian S. F. Platonov suggested was the pattern of Russian history, namely, that the breakdown of a system of rule is ultimately followed by the reconstitution of a new form of state power, perhaps based on key elements of the old, and most importantly, featuring a new army some years later as the true incarnation of that new state power.[37] Yet today that process remains incomplete, given the incompletion of the current defense reform. Indeed, from today's vantage point, we cannot be certain what kind of army Russia will have and whether or not it can adequately defend the state and the regime against foreign or other threats to security. Nonetheless, we cannot gainsay the scope of the current long-term defense modernization program that is currently underway.

Putin's innovative emphasis on economic reconstruction above other considerations goes against the fundamental historical tendencies of Russian statecraft that repeatedly sacrificed the economy to the military and the pursuit of a great power. Yet he also has set in motion a process by which the purpose of this economic development is not growth in and of itself, or for its own sake, but to serve as the foundation for an ambitious global policy based on Russia's supposedly inherent great power status and a quest for independence from all foreign policy constraint. This policy logically entails substantially increased military spending and greater emphasis on defense threats and issues that is more nearly characteristic of Russian history. Worse, it inevitably contributes to the spread of great power tensions along military lines, some of which are already beginning to surface, e.g., the U.S. European Command's earlier demand for more troops in Europe at least in part because of an unpredictable situation in Russia and the growing disposition of certain sectors of the U.S. military to see Russia as a potential future threat, especially as regards nuclear weapons.[38]

Moreover, the jury is still out concerning the ultimate purpose and "destination" of those policies, given the large military buildup underway and the steady and large increases in defense spending. This does not mean that the primacy of the military has been the only tradition. Examples like those of Mikhail Reutern under Alexander II from 1856-78, Count Sergei Witte in 1892-1900, and Peter Stolypin, who was in effect Prime Minister and Minister of Interior from 1906-11, display episodes or cases where the economic reconstruction of Russia took priority or where financial and economic imperatives kept military policy in relative check. Similarly, the New Economic Policy (NEP) of the 1920s and even the first 5-year plan to some degree aimed at economic reconstruction or breakthrough rather than at prioritizing the defense sector. Nonetheless, the priority of defense and foreign policy over Russia's economic health was a trademark of the Tsarist, Stalinist, and post-Stalinist systems and in the Soviet period revealed the logic of Leninism as applied to international politics. Military spending was prioritized because the regime saw the Soviet state as being in a permanent situation of war against domestic "class" enemies and abroad against "imperialism" while it was in a seemingly permanent condition of backwardness. Therefore, the economy and the state had to be permanently mobilized. Consequently, the Soviet economy was "a *sui generis* war economy" in the words of the Polish economist Oskar Lange. That certainly is not the case today, or at least is not yet the case today. But it could come back tomorrow, especially in a system characterized by entropy and reversion to past models of governance as increasingly now seems to be the case.

THE HISTORICAL APPROACH AND THE RESTORATION OF AUTOCRACY

In this context, we seek to analyze and assess contemporary Russian foreign policy as part of Russian history, i.e., through the lens of what historian Alfred Rieber has called "the persistent problems" of Russian foreign policy.[39] But to do so, we must first discuss the nature of the contemporary Russian state. Indeed, as this writer has argued before, Russian foreign and defense policy (i.e., its overall national security policy) directly derives from the nature of the state. Therefore, to grasp the nature of that state, we must go beyond the insufficient contemporary theories to see today's state in its historical context. Here, we must point out that we do not say that Russia's state and foreign policy are mere replicas of the past. Russian foreign and domestic policies are by no means historically determined. But the Russian elites made a conscious choice during the 1990s and that choice, to replicate the historical formation of autocracy, has had consequences in foreign policy. As David Cameron and Mitchell Orenstein recently observed:

> The erosion of rights, liberties, and democracy that has occurred in Russia over the past decade is most frequently associated with the presidency of Vladimir Putin. But there is good reason to believe that the causes of that erosion lie deeper, in the institutional structures of the state, and that whatever erosion of rights, liberties, and democracy occurred during the Putin presidency only continued a process that began during the presidency of his predecessor.[40]

Specifically, this trend is attributable to the outcome of the battle between President Boris Yeltsin and the Duma in 1992-93, a struggle that ended in a violent conflict in Moscow and with the establishment of what amounted to an unfettered and thus autocratic presidency under Yeltsin, who quite consciously liked to be seen as a traditional Russian boss and Tsar.[41]

There are those misguided U.S. analysts who have the bizarre and quite unfounded idea that U.S. writing on Russia suggests that Russian imperialism and anti-Americanism is somehow historically determined.[42] Instead of such misguided and uninformed analysis, we would do better to realize that while today's Russian foreign policy is entangled with Russian history, it also is very much the product of conscious elite strategies based on the interaction of domestic and foreign conditions, elites, and other factors (as is U.S. foreign policy). Marx was right. While men make history, they do not do so as they please but rather under the circumstances bequeathed to them from the past. Consequently, it is entirely arguable that the decision to reconstruct the Russian state along lines based on Russian history is the primary, though hardly the sole, reason for Russia's enduring antagonism to the West, neo-imperial policies towards the CIS, and the suspicion with which many other governments view Russian policy today.

This mutual suspicion is, in no small measure due to the fact that the construction of such a state necessarily implies a presupposition of hostility from all of its interlocutors. As one 2008 analysis observed, "An atmosphere of tension and suspicion towards foreign interests has been crucial to the economic and administrative expansion of the Siloviki, and they will resist attempts to dispel it."[43] Indeed, the study of Russian foreign policy history makes clear that, to Russia, any integration of Europe, as such, has been an enemy threat. This made perfect sense with regard to Napoleonic France and to Hohenzollern and Nazi Germany. But a democratic debellicized Europe integrated in the North Atlantic Treaty Organization (NATO) and the EU, with the latter's emphasis on negating power politics, represents no threat to Russia unless we or Russia proclaim that democracy and the renunciation of unfettered sovereignty — the two hallmarks of contemporary Europe — are in their essence threats to the patrimonial state *Ab Initio*. It should also be pointed out that ultimately the nature of the European project and its emphasis on civil power and democratic, pacific values is utterly incompatible with spheres of influence, neo-imperial power plays, and the corruption of European governing institutions that are all hallmarks of Russian policy.

Interestingly enough, some Russian writers celebrate this inheritance by the state of its patrimonial form and the accompanying historical legacy that the decision to accept this poisoned chalice has extended. Oksana V. Goncharova, of the Russian Public administration, thus writes:

> Russian foreign policy of today is dependent on a lot of factors, including the right use of historic experience. Restoration of the continuity of Russian foreign policy broken by the October Coup of 1917 is the primary goal of those involved in international affairs of the Russian state. The solution of the task will be the formulation of the national idea which the politically active and patriotic segment of Russian society needs, and which would make a solid basis for the national consensus in fundamental foreign policy issues.[44]

Vyacheslav Nikonov writes that, "Something else that is an extremely important thing and distinguishes

Russia from the other powers is that we have preserved the important resource of our historical heritage. With all the revolutionary changes, its historical matrix was reproduced."[45] That matrix is the patrimonial state. Russian elite thinking about Russia's domestic and international position in a world of states and other international actors and about the nature of the policies it should therefore conduct is also decisively shaped and influenced by, and even enmeshed to a considerable degree in, Russian history. Indeed, its progenitors explicitly invoke that history, e.g., Putin's aforementioned essay of January 2012 that explicitly invokes a famous quotation from the Tsarist Foreign Minister A. M. Gorchakov and openly appeals to Russian history to justify his course, Sergei Ivanov's remarks below, and former Foreign Minister and Prime Minister Evgeny Primakov's and other analysts' appeal to Gorchakov's struggle after the Crimean War to reassert Russia's power in Europe.[46] More recently, Putin seems to have wrapped himself up in the mantle of Petr Stolypin; Nicholas II's last reforming Prime Minister (1906-11). Meanwhile President Medvedev tried to cast himself in the mold of the Tsar Liberator, Alexander II.[47] Putin's success in invoking, incarnating, and reconfirming Russia's great power position is bound up not only with his ever tightening control of the media to drown out competing narratives and opinions, but also with the fact that he appealed to and appeared to incarnate to a considerable degree a historically shaped identity and personal role that were perceived to be clearly in danger upon his arrival on the scene.[48]

Therefore Russia arguably presents itself to the world as a kind of *"Monstre Sacree"* ("sacred monster") to invoke the French term. Russia still tends to see itself as a sacred or at least privileged and unique state with a special path (*Osobyi Put'*) not bound by the usual rules of international activity and demands that others accept this self-valuation as their valuation of Russia. It projects autocratic unlimited power into the international arena as a justification of its unfettered sovereignty and right to do as it pleases regardless of international law, practice, or any other constraint. Meanwhile, its interlocutors still frequently also see it as a monster intent on dominating, if not trampling, the neighborhood.

At the same time this phrase, "sacred monster" connotes the self-perception of a singular entity that demands that others accord it the status it claims for itself, i.e., its undisputed right to be above any form of international accountability. For example, the Russian government in the person of Foreign Minister Lavrov most recently basically told the world that it does not have to account to anyone for sending a ship laden with ammunition to Syria to assist the government in murdering protesters.[49] Russia's belief that it is beyond accounting to any state or institution's norms, which are in any case simply an expression of a strong state's interest, not any kind of objective moral value, transfers Russian domestic values into Russian foreign policy. Indeed, it places those domestic values at the heart of foreign policy as an object that is under attack and must be defended by a pervasive threat. Thus Timofei Bordachev, a Europe specialist at the prestigious Council on Foreign and Defense Policy (SVOP), wrote that a new format for developing Russo-EU relations must acknowledge Russia's special role in the world and should therefore not relate to any past EU partnership and cooperation agreements with anyone else. Any agreement with Russia must be unique, reflecting Russia's undefined, but taken for granted, uniqueness. Second, the new agreement cannot be a kind of European lesson plan for Russia, instructing it how drawing it closer to Europe by postulating reformed regulatory political and economic policies. Russia cannot adopt EU legislation or standards if it is not to become a member of the EU (even if they would immensely benefit Russia) for that allegedly makes no sense. Third, "any new document between the parties must avoid evaluative judgment of the Russian economy and its society as a whole." Russia must remain beyond any foreign or other evaluation.[50]

Thus Moscow regards Russia's internal structure as a point of contestation that must be removed from the agenda of world politics. On the one hand, this patrimonial structure is integral to the establishment of a great and feared power, even empire.

> In practical terms, this means a "Conservative change" later translated into restoration of the famous power *Vertikal*, the taking over of competitive private enterprises by state companies, maintenance of natural monopolies economic and political instruments of government, reform of armed forces, social protection system, banking and financial sectors. Russia's internal agenda represents a constitutive part of a plan designated to reclaim the great power status on the international arena.[51]

Obviously this system must be protected from foreign attacks. It must be free from having to answer for its behavior, and Russian leaders must obtain that freedom of action through their conduct of foreign policy. Arguably, they have succeeded to a considerable degree. In 2009, Arkady Moshes of the Finnish Institute of International Relations observed that:

As far as European actors are concerned, the following moments have to be taken into consideration. First, in the middle of the current decade Russia has successfully taken its internal order off the Russian-European agenda. With the help of a rather influential European school of thought, Moscow effectively promoted the line of being an 'imperfect democracy' and lobbied for the prioritization of pragmatic interests over liberal values. Whereas the question whether or not Europe's consent not to lecture Russia on its internal affairs helped the former to pursue those interests remains largely rhetorical, Moscow got an impression that in reality values did not matter for Europe. Rather, they were a bargaining chip, which could be traded for economic or other concessions.[52]

Not surprisingly, many Russian political figures see the state as essentially traditional. Mikhail Gorbachev recently said that the Stalinist system is still being partially used in Russia.[53] Semyon Novoprudsky sees the state as bearing enormous resemblances to its Soviet predecessor throughout the state structure, and even in the society.[54] Dmitry Furman observed that, "managed democracies are actually a soft variant of the Soviet system."[55] Moreover, Russian patrimonialism and autocracy probably cannot survive without replicating itself in Ukraine and across the CIS. Thus it is hardly surprising that Medvedev, like Putin and Yeltsin before him, has now formally claimed an undefined sphere of influence going beyond the old Soviet borders as a fundamental principle of Russian foreign policy.[56] Celeste Wallander, now Deputy Assistant Secretary of Defense, called this transimperialism, although the label is less important than the imperialistic reality.

Transimperialism is the extension of Russian patrimonial authoritarianism into a globalized world. Russia
can trade and invest without being open and permeable by selectively integrating transnational elite networks in the globalized international economic system
and replicating the patron-client relations of power,
dependency, and rent seeking and distribution at the
transnational level. Russian foreign policy is increasingly founded on creating transnational elite networks
for access to rent-creating opportunities in the globalized international economy. Moscow functions as
the arbiter and control point for Russia's interaction
with the outside economy to ensure that Russia is not
exposed to the liberalizing effects of marketization,
competition, and diversification of interests and local
power. If that were to happen, the political system that
keeps the present leadership in power would be at risk
of failing. In this sense, globalization is a threat not to
Russian national interests but to the interests of Russia's political leadership.[57]

Both NATO and EU enlargement to Ukraine represent this kind of globalization. Accordingly, the reform
of Ukraine's politics, and in particular Ukraine's enormously corrupt gas trading operations with Russia,
is a critical component of Ukraine's integration with
the West and the rest of the world. This corrupt trade
and Ukraine's undefined political trajectory are foundations of Russia's autocracy and efforts to corrupt
Western public institutions and politicians through
the use of energy in tandem with organized crime, the
Russian state, and intelligence agencies.[58] Thus this
strategy, in its energy and military dimensions, aims
to stop the threat posed by European integration in
its tracks, or to limit the damage to what has already
been lost and, if possible, reverse it by hollowing out
the institutions of European unification as Medvedev
noted above.[59]

Effectively Moscow aims to undo in practice the content of the post-Soviet and former Warsaw Pact states' sovereignty. Michael Emerson of the Center for European Policy Studies in Brussels, Belgium, reports the comments of a civil society leader in Belarus who told him that, "we have the impression that Moscow has come to see a certain Finlandization of Belarus as unavoidable and even useful."[60] As Emerson describes the term, Finlandization means:

> Remaining in Moscow's orbit for strategic security affairs (strategic military installations, 50% ownership of the gas pipeline, no question of NATO aspirations), but becoming more open to its EU neighbors for personal contacts and eventual political liberalization and for modernizing its economy. All this has the ring of plausibility to it.[61]

While this may look attractive to Moscow or maybe even to some of the governments of the region like Belarus and Armenia, and possibly Moldova, it clearly does not satisfy Ukraine and probably Azerbaijan, not to mention Georgia, or leave any of these states with full sovereignty over their foreign, defense, and economic policies. According to Emerson even if none of those post-Soviet states currently has a credible prospect for either the EU or NATO, Russia's multi-dimensional presence is either sustained or growing throughout the region.[62]

Although some American analysts like Thomas Graham have recommended Ukraine's Finlandization as a goal of U.S. policy, it is quite unlikely, given Ivanov's and many others' statements, that Moscow really looks forward to these states' political liberalization and enhanced contacts with the EU; quite the contrary.[63] In other words, Moscow has rather a different definition of Finlandization, one that is much more politically and economically restrictive. Meanwhile, in Central and Eastern Europe Moscow wants "trojan horses" inside the EU and NATO. For example, upon Bulgaria's accession to the EU in 2007, Russian Ambassador to the EU Vladimir Chizhov publicly said that Bulgaria was Moscow's trojan horse there, and in 2008 stated that Russia counted on Bulgaria and other states to block sanctions against it in the wake of the 2008 war with Georgia.[64] Certainly NATO as well as the EU regarded the Dimitrov government in Bulgaria that was in power until earlier in 2009 as little more than just such a trojan horse.[65]

Moreover, close examination of Russian policies throughout Eastern Europe as defined here indicates that Moscow's aims go beyond those listed by Emerson. The multiplicity of incidents we have listed here or that others like Keith Smith, Robert Larsson, Anita Orban, and Janusz Bugajski *et al.*, have listed indicate that we are witnessing a coordinated Russian strategy directed against Europe.[66] As a recent assessment of Russian policy in Latvia concluded:

> We see several, interrelated short-term [Russian] strategies focusing on exercising ever-increasing influence in the politics of the target states. What we do not see is a policy of military conquest but, rather, a gradual but unswerving drive to eventually regain dominance over the social, economic, and political affairs of what are to become entirely dependent client states.[67]

NORMATIVE OR IDEOLOGICAL FACTORS
IN RUSSIAN POLICY

Here we must realize that, Igor Ivanov's writings aside, contemporary international politics is once again or perhaps never stopped being ideological as well as geopolitical and geoeconomic. Not even Trenin's Russians are ready to get up in public and say they recognize nothing but power and interest. Thus Moscow's foreign policy approach, especially in the former Soviet borderlands, becomes an ideological-political one as acknowledged by both foreign and Russian observers. Temur Basilia, Special Assistant to former Georgian President Edvard Shevarnadze for economic issues, wrote that in many CIS countries, e.g., Georgia and Ukraine, "the acute issue of choosing between alignment with Russia and the West is associated with the choice between two models of social development."[68] The aptness of this observation transcends Georgia and Ukraine to embrace the entire post-Soviet region, since it is clear that Moscow viscerally opposes "exporting democracy" to it. Indeed, it regards the idea with contempt and thus attracts the local dictators who cleave to it for support against Western pressures for democratization.[69] Basilia also pointed to the local perception of Russia as a security threat.

> Nowadays there are many in the West who believe that Russia has changed — and, having reformed, seeks to interact with neighboring countries in conformity with international norms. Some Eurasian countries would disagree with this opinion, and believe instead that the Russian mentality has not changed much, and that Russia continues to deem the "near abroad" as its sphere of social influence. After the second war with

Chechnya, many think that Russia regards violence as its major tool for resolving social and political problems, especially with regard to non-Russian peoples from the former empire. Thus integration into the international community should be viewed as a guarantee for security and further development.[70]

Similarly Sabine Fischer writes:

Ukraine's foreign policy orientation does not only involve a choice between different partners for political and economic cooperation. It is a strategic decision between two models of development, and as such essentially a decision on the identity and future of the country. It forms part of Ukraine's state and nation-building processes, and its outcome will have a decisive impact on the future of the region, and Europe in general.[71]

Finally, Lilia Shevtsova reminds us that:

No matter whether the Russian foreign policy takes the form of a dialogue or confrontation with the West, its aim remains to keep in place a personalized power system that is inherently hostile to liberal democracy. The optimists who get excited every time the Kremlin starts cooperating with Western partners would do well to remember this.[72]

Russian analysts like the late Dmitry Furman also acknowledge that "The Russia-West struggle in the CIS is a struggle between two irreconcilable systems."[73] Furman's analysis is instructive of the regime's compelling need for a foreign policy enemy that seeks not only to weaken Russia but to block its full return to great power status, particularly in the CIS.

Our system's democratic camouflage demands partnership with the West. However, the authoritarian, managed content of our system dictates the exact opposite. A safety zone for our system means a zone of political systems of the same kind of managed democracies that we are actively supporting in the CIS and, insofar as our forces allow, everywhere — in Serbia, the Middle East, even Venezuela. The Soviet Union's policy might seem quixotic. Why spend so much money in the name of 'proletarian internationalism'? But if you do not expand, you contract. The same could be said about our policy toward Lukashenko's regime [in Belarus-author]. The system of managed democracy in Russia will perish if Russia is besieged on all sides by unmanaged democracies. Ultimately it will once again be a matter of survival. The West cannot fail to support the establishment of systems of the same type as the West's, which means expanding its safety zone. We cannot fail to oppose this. Therefore the struggle inside the CIS countries is beginning to resemble the Russian-Western conflict.[74]

THE PERSISTENT PROBLEMS OF RUSSIAN HISTORY

Rieber's approach emphasizing the persistent problems of Russian history originated in his dissatisfaction with the pieties and clichés of earlier generations of Russian historiography and of foreign historiography about Russia. But it also represented an effort to find satisfying answers to what are also discernible persisting continuities in Russian history up to the end of the Soviet period and more recently to the present even under conditions of profound revolutionary change.[75] Any worthwhile account of this history must account for both the continuities, most visible in the continuing form of rule, i.e., the Muscovite or Tsarist

paradigm of autocracy described here, and the rup-
tures like the revolutions of 1917 and 1991. This Muscovite or Tsarist paradigm is characterized by the government's or the Tsar's control, even ownership of the
national economy; the absence of enforceable property
rights, public, legal, or Parliamentary controls on the
government; the absence of the rule of law, a strong
tendency towards emphasizing the military or martial
aspects of national security policy over other dimensions; a quasi-militarized state rhetoric, if not concept
of the state's organization; a caesaro-papist ideology
making the ruler the object of cultic veneration; and
an accompanying great power and imperial mystique
as well as reality. One major purpose of that imperial
mystique and its accompanying reality is to translate
these domestic factors into international factors to
ensure the security of this inherently insecure and illegitimate (in contemporary European and Western
terms) regime.

The state in this paradigm was also, as were the
Tsarist and Stalinist states, a service state in which everyone was bound to serve the state and power as well
as income, especially at the top of society, only came
from the rewards of service. Just as the "Boyars" must
serve in order to gain control over the rents coming
from the state and are thus a rent-seeking elite, so too
the state grants these rents with the proviso that they
serve the Tsar well (even if corruptly). Hence the state
is a rent-granting state and the elite a rent-seeking
elite. Today the service state is still far too present (not
just in the army still subject to conscription, but also in
the government). To cite one example, in a notorious
late 2007 interview, Oleg Shvartsman, a "businessman" admitted that he was the front for an interlock-
ing series of organizations representing high-ranking
government figures and their families that raided cor-

porations to take them over on behalf of his "clients" and their families. Shvartsman further admitted that the government had set up an organization at Putin's direction in 2004 to compel businesses to be "more socially responsible" and that it engaged in what he called "collective blackmail."[76] Similarly, we see the large role of so-called informal taxes, i.e., demands by the state and Kremlin for contributions outside the formal system of taxes and other rule-based obligations.[77] The Kremlin's ongoing expropriation of foreign and domestic businessmen who run afoul of it, most recently expressed in its late summer of 2011 raids against British Petroleum (BP) is another example of a government who feels that all the property belongs to it, that it can seize that property whenever it suits it to do so, and that this is nobody else's affair. All these manifestations of state expropriation and compulsory service as a condition of possessing property and/or political position derive from the medieval phenomena of such taxes, predatory confiscation of estates, and *krugovaya poruka* (collective surety).

In less stringent times, e.g., after the emancipation of the serfs, the obligation to serve was partially relaxed, but it is clear in Putin's Russia that his topmost elites are state servants in exactly the same way as were Tsarist or Soviet officials.[78] That is, they retain their office and property on the basis of their loyal service to Putin or Medvedev, a service that exempts them from true legal accountability to anyone or any institution and enables them to retain their access to rents throughout the system that are obtained by a pervasive corruption. Absent legal and institutional checks upon the power of the autocrat, rival bureaucracies emerge out of rival factions and clans at court, and the Tsar's task is to check each group by the other, while remaining in some sense above the fray, not least through the mystique of Tsardom and the cult of personality. Or as Clifford Gaddy observes, the Tsar is the ultimate arbiter of rents.[79] But as all good histories of Tsarist Russia show, this resembles the political function of the later Tsars who constantly were balancing off factions around them, each of whom wanted preeminence and unimpeded direct access to the Tsar. Much the same behavior is also observable among Soviet General Secretaries, including Stalin. Even though his power was as absolute as anyone could wish for, he was constantly balancing off competing factions in his Politburo and cabinet. Policy thus often emerges out of the strife of these bureaucratic and "courtly" factions.

But given the pervasive corruption, patron-client relationships, and endless rivalry of courtiers for the favor of the Tsar (or president), the end result is a blurring of the distinction between personal and national interest and thus persistent, endemic, and structurally rooted, as well as culturally permitted corruption on a grand scale. Indeed, given the interpenetration of officialdom and business, it is often all but impossible to distinguish between the motives of each side in foreign policy deals. It becomes clear that it is equally difficult to distinguish between the personal or sectoral interests of actors and the national interest for each of those conceptions of interest is, as James Sherr, notes, "a primary color" that must be combined in the overall picture to be seen properly.[80] Such features typify the authoritarian and backward state. The following observations about Afghanistan could be literally word-for-word true about Russia.

The structural lack of competition and representation has significant ramifications for performance, for it inhibits accountability and pushes political competition outside the formal, legal system, where it has taken the form of informal contests for patronage and the capture of resources. The formal rules of the game become meaningless, and performance by state officials becomes transactional rather than rational.[81]

Therefore, the personal interest of elite members often, if not always, trumps any true concept of national interest. We see examples of this and of the rivalry between competing bureaucracies, elites, and factions, with particular vividness in the energy sector. For example, Russia and China have been discussing oil and gas pipelines for years to no avail. Indeed, in 2003-08 the issue was whether to go with a pipeline to China alone or to the Pacific Ocean coast and Japan.

In reality, it is not China or Japan, but Russia that wants to bring large volumes of its oil and gas to the market of Northeast Asia in the most economical way. Also, it is not Japan and China who are the main contenders for a pipeline route, but rather diverse interests within Russia. Indeed, some interest groups would prefer to explore the oil and natural gas reserves in a way that would not necessarily gain local industries and communities, and without considering the overall groups that prioritize regional developments, social advancement and national energy markets, as well as access to multiple markets in Northeast Asia. The problem is that the Chinese decided to side with the former, while the Japanese aimed towards the latter. Tokyo was only supporting, not proposing the pipeline route that Transneft already advocated and that President Putin strongly favored.[82]

Consequently, the competition for pipeline routes and financing in Asia was as much an internal Russian factional fight for rents, bribes, and influence as it was a foreign policy strategy. Russia's ultimate decision clearly reflected the personal interests of key bureaucratic players, who prevailed at the expense of the earlier policy and concept of Russian national interest. Then in 2009 at the bottom of the financial crisis, Igor Sechin and Sergei Bogdanchikov, the heads of Rosneft and Transneft, pushed through loans from China to their organizations on condition that they build an oil pipeline to China, which opened in 2011. But they did so under conditions that undercut Russian national interests, which called for a pipeline to more than one customer. At the same time, they undermined the Russian railways, which had previously carried the oil to China in return for a handsome Chinese subsidy. It is difficult to imagine that their motive was not as much bureaucratic and personal as it was supposedly in the national interest, for Russia still is hobbled in the Far East with regard to energy sales to Japan, South Korea, and other potential buyers.

Similar examples exist in the struggle over foreign arms purchases. While it is clear that the Russian defense industry cannot provide the quality and high-tech weapons demanded and needed by the military, it and its bureaucratic patrons refuse to let go of the rents accruing to them and insist against all reason and evidence that they can do better. This is not just (although it is in part) nationalist boasting.[83] These examples therefore indicate to us the continuing saliency of historic Russian structures, mentalities, and behavior patterns: imperialism, a particular kind of militarism, factional rivalry, and the continuation of the autocratic state and its particular mentality.

If we view this collective elite mentality and behavior of the elite at home and abroad in the light of this historical inheritance, we encounter a revived form of the essence of the Soviet *Nomenklatura*, namely the medieval and feudal fusion of power and property, along with feudal patron-client relationships and many elements of the service state. In other words, a great deal of medievalism still attaches itself to Russian politics at home and abroad. In the light of such episodes as those recounted by Shvartsman and, for example, the Magnitsky and Khodorkovsky affairs, it becomes clear why foreign diplomats and officials, including the U.S. embassy have labeled Russia a "mafia state."[84] Clifford Gaddy and Barry Ickes called Putin's system a protection racket some time ago.[85] Even former Russian officials have done the same thing. As Andrei Illarionov testified to Congress in 2009:

> According to the classification of the political regimes, the current one in Russia should be considered as hard authoritarianism. The central place in the Russian political system is occupied by the Corporation of the secret police. The personnel of Federal Security Service—both in active service as well as retired one—form a special type of unity (non-necessarily institutionalized) that can be called *brotherhood, order,* or *corporation*. The Corporation of the secret police operatives (CSP) includes first of all acting and former officers of the FSB (former KGB), and to a lesser extent FSO and Prosecutor General Office. Officers of GRU and SVR do also play some role. The members of the Corporation do share strong allegiance to their respective organizations, strict codes of conduct and of honor, basic principles of behavior, including among others the principle of mutual support to each other in any circumstances and the principle of *omerta*. Since the Corporation preserves traditions, hierarchies,

codes and habits of secret police and intelligence services, its members show high degree of obedience to the current leadership, strong loyalty to each other, rather strict discipline. There are both formal and informal means of enforcing these norms. Violators of the code of conduct are subject to the harshest forms of punishment, including the highest form.[86]

What this means, and the second conviction of Mikhail Khodorkovsky in December 2010 confirms, is that executive power is undivided, the courts cannot check it, there is no unconditional right of property, no truly enforceable contracts by recourse to impartial law costs, and the state leadership is determined to keep things this way. Its Mafia-like qualities testify to the fact that force is the ultimate arbiter of all decisions, that rivalries for control of property and power dominate the state, and that the regime refuses to subject itself to any legal accountability so that those who cannot be bribed or simply intimidated are subjected to force *majeure* or killed. Likewise, we see the control by members of the government of the major engines of economic activity and the use of unbridled and unaccountable state power to oust rivals from the scene. These state megaliths have grown, thanks to state cronyism and systematic predation, not excluding officially sponsored corporate raiding.

Indeed, as Khodorkovsky observed, corruption is probably Russia's greatest export, much as in a criminal racket. We see this not only in Ukraine's notorious corruption or the similar phenomena in Central Asia, but also in countless examples in Eastern Europe. Thus events and trends in Central and Eastern Europe fully display the linkages between energy firms, intelligence penetration, efforts to buy up strategic sectors of the local economy, influence peddling, corruption, and the buying and subversion of politicians and political institutions that we see across Europe and that can only be part of a centrally directed Russian policy to achieve the objectives stated above of eroding European security and democracy.

Simultaneously, European intelligence services and NATO have discerned a vast expansion of the Russian intelligence network in Europe and its efforts to penetrate and destabilize European governments. These trends are particularly noticeable at NATO headquarters in Brussels and in Eastern Europe. The head of Polish Military Intelligence, Antoni Macierewicz, observed in 2007 that Poland was under attack from a greatly expanded covert network of agents.[87] In 2008 Vladimir Fillin, the Ukraine office chief of forum. msk, told a gathering of Ukrainian law-enforcement officials that:

> For some time now the Ukrainian special services have been discharging the country's international commitments by working actively to curb smuggling that is 'sheltered' by influential Chekist forces in the Russian Federation. The Chekists have taken over Russia's internal heroin and cocaine market and are now trying to expand as far as they can into the Ukrainian and European markets. . . . However nothing has come of their efforts.[88]

In July 2009 Kyiv expelled two Russian diplomats from the Crimea, not for spying, which would be bad enough, but unfortunately something we all live with. Rather, they were trying to incite the population against the Ukrainian government.[89]

We find analogous examples in Poland, the Baltic, Hungary, and the Czech Republic, if not elsewhere in Central and Eastern Europe. For example, in 2004 Roman Giertych, Deputy Chairman of the commission that investigated the notorious Orlen scandal in Poland, concluded in his report that:

> The commission has evidence that a certain kind of conspiracy functioned "within the background of the State Treasury Ministry, the Prime Ministerial Chancellery, the Presidential Chancellery, and big business," which was supposed to bring about the sale of the Polish energy sector into the hands of Russian firms.[90]

In Lithuania, former President Rolandas Paskas was impeached for his connections to Russian organized crime and intelligence figures. As of August 2009, the Seimas was moving to block any possibility that the Russo-Lithuanian capital bank Snoras could gain control of the Lieutvos Rytas media group.[91] But this is hardly a new Russian policy.

In 2007-08, Lithuanian businessman Rimandas Stonys, President of Dujotekana, Lithuania's Gazprom intermediary, who has close ties to Russian and Lithuanian officials and has extensive investments in Lithuania's energy and transit sectors, was brought under investigation by Lithuania's Parliament. These investigative reports charge that he had used his ties to Russian intelligence and other Lithuanian political connections to advance personal and Russian interests in Lithuania's energy sector. Dujotekana is reputed to be a front for Russian intelligence services that are already entwined with Gazprom. A counterintelligence probe into a foreign citizen's efforts to recruit senior Lithuanian Intelligence (VSD) officers led to the firm, which also recruited government officials. Key executives of Dujotekana are apparently also KGB alumni. Similar charges are also raised in regard to Stonys' and his firm's influence in Lithuania's transit sector and his large contributions to politicians and media and his influence over political appointments.[92]

Since then, it has become clear that the company was established with the help of Russian special services, but because Stonys failed to gain control of a new power plant in Kaunas that would have legitimized Gazprom as an investor and power in Lithuania, he may well be on his way out.[93] However, that would hardly stop other friends of Russia from trying to capture key positions in the state and its policy.[94] Indeed, Gazprom is still trying to obtain a long-term contract to supply Lithuania with gas and make a deal with the main gas company, Lieutvos Dujos, until 2030. [95] Clearly, this is a constant, long-term Russian policy. Thus Stonys only took off from where earlier efforts had failed when attempts were made to compromise Lithuanian politics by using such figures as Viktor Uspaskich, founder of the Labor party, who is trying to make a comeback, and Paskas.[96] Likewise, in Estonia, the 2006 annual report of the Security Police noted that the Constitution Party is financed partly from Moscow.[97]

In Hungary, Istvan Simiscko, a member of the Christian Democratic People's Party and Chairman of the National Security Committee of the Parliament, has publicly charged that Russian (and possibly Slovak) intelligence and criminal links may be involved in the murder of members of the Hungarian Roma in an attempt to incite ethnic unrest inside Hungary and/or discredit Hungary abroad.[98] There are also repeated examples of Russia, either acting on its own or through the Austrian energy firm OMV, attempting to gain control over Hungarian energy firms, notably MOL.[99] Thus there has been good reason for open

U.S. concern about Hungarian policy, especially when the Socialists led by Prime Minister Ferenc Gyurcany were in power.[100] Indeed, Gyurcsany had, at various times, proposed that the EU, Russia, and Caspian Sea governments form an energy partnership or said that, despite Hungary's democratic orientation, it cannot expect to become independent of Russia.[101] More recently, there are discernible signs of this phalanx of business, crime, and government money establishing havens for itself in Iceland and Montenegro.[102] In other words, we are confronting a pervasive and strategic policy on the part of the Russian elite to corrupt European public institutions.

However, the most comprehensive recent example occurred in the Czech Republic. Prague's recent expulsion of two Russian diplomats, including the defense attaché, for spying has revealed the scope of the problem even though Moscow, as is its habit, denounced the charges as provocations. Diplomats have stated that Russia is increasing its network in Prague to the extent of activating sleepers or past agents and reverting to Soviet methods. For some time, the Czechs have been investigating this expansion of Russian intelligence, subversion, and espionage activity, thanks to the arrest in 2008 of Herman Simm, a high-ranking Estonian official in the Ministry of Interior who was a Russian spy. As one NATO diplomat told the Czech newspaper *Mlada Fronta Dnes*:

> The extensive building up of Russian espionage networks in the Czech Republic and in other NATO countries, and also the hitherto unprecedented amounts of money that Moscow was starting to invest in this 'project' in the recent period have exceeded the acceptable, and sometimes also tolerated, limits of espionage, . . . In the recent period this has exceeded any kind of

degree, whether this is a case of infiltrating the intelligence services or of contacting experts involved in NATO strategic defense.[103]

What reportedly most disconcerted NATO about these trends is not the intelligence gained by Moscow, but the fact that Russia has returned to Soviet practices and clearly views NATO as enemy number one.[104] Had NATO paid closer attention to Russian statements and policy, it would not have been surprised. Formally, Prague expelled these diplomats for attempting to influence public opinion against the planned U.S. missile defense installations in the Czech Republic. Czech officials and reports have long observed that, using business and either Czech or Russian businessmen as a front, Moscow has been trying to make contact with and suborn politicians to influence Czech policies.

Moscow has doubled the number of known agents in the Czech Republic from 50-100, and many officials believe that the leadership of the Czech Social Democratic party is either prey to dangerous illusions about Russia or worse and would undermine Prague's pro-Western policies.[105] A report from Radio Free Europe indicates that an increasing number of Czech politicians have ties to Russia in one form or another, including state-owned Russian enterprises in which energy enterprises figure prominently.[106] Most of these firms operate by stealth like the gas trading firm Vemex that controls 12 percent of the Czech domestic market and which is controlled by the Centrex Group Ltd., whose official ownership is impossible to trace but is one of Gazprom's East and Central European firms set up to muscle into the European utilities business. Likewise, Lukoil has enormous pull inside the Czech Republic and has secured preferential contracts to provide oil and jet fuel to Czech concerns and the Prague airport. There is good reason to believe that these business activities are also transferring money to Czech political groups.[107] Czech intelligence thus reports that Russian intelligence has attempted to establish and exploit ties to Czech politicians and civic groups for purposes hostile to government policy and on behalf of Russia.[108] As one representative of Czech Intelligence, the BIS, told the Czech journal *Respekt.cz* previously:

> In the last few years we have noted numerous attempts by business entities that had proven connections to suspicious Russian capital to gain control over telecommunications, information systems, and transportation infrastructure from railroads to airports and airlines. To what extent the Russian secret services are involved in these activities, however, we do not know.[109]

Knowledgeable Czech experts like the former Ambassador to Moscow Lucas Dobrovsky have little doubt what Moscow wants to achieve through such efforts to penetrate the Czech government. As he observed:

> We would stop resisting the efforts to bring Russia's economic, political, and perhaps, to a certain extent, military, influence back to the area of Central Europe. The current Russian Government and the president believe that this is a natural influence in the area that was directly and indirectly occupied by the former Soviet Union. You will find a lot of evidence of this in the statements of Russian politicians. This would lead to the weakening of our Euro-Atlantic relations.[110]

Czech Deputy Foreign Minister Thomas Pojar echoes these comments and notes that recovering

Russia's position in Central Europe has been a Putin priority since he took power in 2000.[111]

Apart from Russian efforts to undermine popular support for the stationing of U.S. missile defense radars in the Czech Republic, these espionage activities are clearly connected to Russian efforts to take over and penetrate key sectors of the Czech economy. For example, Russian interests are trying to buy into the nuclear storage sector, an effort that according to intelligence experts immediately raises questions, especially as Russian diplomats are involved in this project.[112] Indeed, the whole question of the tenders for the Temelin nuclear plant, a major project intended to facilitate Czech energy independence, reflect substantial attempts by Russian entities to buy into Temelin and control it. In all these cases as well, we find examples of corruption, price overruns, and criminality ensnaring Russians and Czechs in an intricate web of corruption.[113] Russian agents have likewise repeatedly tried to infiltrate Czech political parties and make contact with members of Parliament, their staffs, and personnel in the foreign relations departments of political parties in order to gain key access to critical economic sectors.

> Shell reportedly wants to sell its 16 percent share in Ceska Rafinerska, a refinery company. One of the main suitors? Supposedly, Russian Lukoil which recently expanded its local network of gas stations. The troubled Polish company PKN Orlen might want to sell its stake in Unipetrol, the Czech company that controls Ceska Rafinerska. The likely suitor? Again the Russians. The list goes on. Such worries about Russian expansion aren't surprising when one considers that the Russian company TVEL will, beginning in 2010, start supplying the Czech nuclear power plant

Temelin with fuel, replacing Westinghouse, the American firm; a Czech subsidiary of the Russian company OMZ will take part in additional work on Temelin; and Gazprom, the Russian gas giant, controls Vermex, the second largest importer of gas from Russia.[114]

Although Russian officials deny interfering in the activities of Russian companies, the record clearly contradicts such denials. So until the charges of economic expansion subside and the opacity characteristic of Russian business-government relations lifts, nobody will believe that the signs of increased Russian activity in the Czech Republic are purely commercial, certainly not the Czechs.[115] Indeed, the criminalization of the energy sector is so great that a Russian newspaper opined that one of the reasons for President Medvedev's violent attacks on Ukraine's government on August 11, 2009, and refusal to send Ambassador Mikhail Zurabov there, is that the attacks also intended to keep Zurabov from gaining control over gas flows through Ukraine, so that the state, not Gazprom, will run the policy and control those flows at the end of the day.[116]

Through such means, Russia tries to corrupt European public institutions, forestall European integration, and remain a wholly free and independent "sovereign democracy" that answers to nobody for its conduct and possesses an unchallenged sphere of influence in countries with which it claims to have "privileged interests."[117] This "damage limitation" posture is inherently revisionist and ultimately opposes the pacification of Europe that is the greatest product and triumph of our times.

SOVEREIGNTY AND DEMOCRACY IN EURASIA

While Russia may have renounced formal empire and territorial expansion, it certainly has not abandoned the autocratic state, its neo-imperial proclivities, many historical mental and behavior patterns, and its assertion of Russian *Samobytnost'* (uniqueness) or revisionist policies in Eurasia. However, if this is the matrix, to use Nikonov's term, from which the current state has issued, it is quite logical that it will be a state whose foreign policy is dominated by the *a priori* presupposition of conflict with its main interlocutors, if not its neighbors as well. There are several reasons for saying this.

As we noted above, one of those resemblances to the Russian historical tradition is the imperial concept of the state, which is expressed in the assertion that, of the post-Soviet successor states, only Russia truly has sovereignty, and those states are in some way artificial, illegitimate, and not truly sovereign. Therefore, Russia is entitled to a sphere of influence in these states, and the consolidation of that sphere is a test of the viability of the state. In other words, as we shall see below, Russian elites believe that if Russia does not have this dominion over those states, it will not only cease to be a great power, but its own statehood will come under question.

For example, in 2008 at the Bucharest NATO-Russia Council on April 4, 2008, President Putin told President Bush, "But, George, don't you understand that Ukraine is not a state." Putin further claimed that most of its territory was a Russian gift in the 1950s. Moreover, while Western Ukraine belonged to Eastern Europe, Eastern Ukraine was "ours." Furthermore, if Ukraine did enter NATO, Russia would then detach

Eastern Ukraine (and the Crimea) and graft it onto Russia. Thus Ukraine would cease to exist as a state.[118] Putin also said that Russia regards NATO enlargement as a threat, so if Georgia received membership, Moscow would "take adequate measures" and recognize Abkhazia and South Ossetia to create a buffer between NATO and Russia.[119] Putin's outburst is not unrepresentative of Russian foreign policy. Instead, it mirrors numerous statements by officials made to former Soviet republics and Eastern European states to the effect that they are not really sovereign states.[120]

On August 11, 2009, Medvedev published an open letter, ostensibly to President Viktor Yushchenko of Ukraine, but actually to the whole country, lambasting Ukraine's policies, announcing that he will withhold sending Ukraine a new ambassador, and calling upon the Ukrainian people to elect a new pro-Russian president.[121] Medvedev specifically charged that:

> The leadership in Kiev took an openly anti-Russian stand following the military attack launched by the Saakashvili regime against South Ossetia. Ukrainian weapons were used to kill civilians and Russian peacekeepers. Russia continues to experience problems caused by a policy aimed at obstructing the operations of its Black Sea Fleet, and this on a daily basis and in violation of the basic agreements between our countries. Sadly, the campaign continues to oust the Russian language from the Ukrainian media, the education, culture and science. The Ukrainian leadership's outwardly smooth-flowing rhetoric fits ill with the overt distortion of complex and difficult episodes in our common history, the tragic events of the great famine in the Soviet Union, and an interpretation of the Great Patriotic War as some kind of confrontation between two totalitarian systems.

Our economic relations are in a somewhat better situation and are developing, but we have not yet succeeded in tapping their full potential. Again, the problem is that Russian companies frequently face open resistance from the Ukrainian authorities. Bypassing Russia, Ukraine's political leaders do deals with the European Union on supplying gas — gas from Russia — and sign a document that completely contradicts the Russian-Ukrainian agreements reached in January this year.[122]

This extraordinarily insulting letter's publication, not to mention its writing, was an overt gesture of contempt towards Ukraine's sovereignty and Yushchenko personally. Its authorship and, *a fortiori*, its publication, fully display to the world that Medvedev shares Putin's assessment of Ukraine's sovereignty and, for that matter, the sovereignty of the other CIS governments. It makes clear that what angers Russia is the idea that Ukraine might actually exercise the prerogatives of an independent sovereign state and demand that Russia not meddle in its politics and elections, uphold the treaty on the Black Sea Fleet, desist from trying to take over Ukraine's energy economy and wage energy wars against it, and come to terms with the Soviet (not just Stalinist) legacy. Thus it is clear that Moscow cannot accept that Ukraine as a sovereign state may decide its foreign policy independently. Instead, if Ukraine is not neutral on behalf of Russia, its sovereignty will come under Russian assault.[123]

Nor is this attitude restricted to Ukraine. At least since 2007, Moscow's true aim is Georgian "neutrality," i.e., a renunciation of its sovereign pro-Western orientation and a further abridgement of its sovereignty.[124] Indeed, it pervades official thinking and rhetoric about the former Soviet bloc, not just the Soviet Union.[125] As Dmitri Trenin recently acknowledged, "as an international actor, Russia is at a point where it recognizes all former borderland republics as separate countries, even if it does not yet see all of them as foreign states."[126] Indeed, Russian ambassadors and officials, taking their cue, perhaps, from Putin's remarks to President Bush, often publicly display their belief that post-Soviet states and even the smaller states of Eurasia are not really true sovereign states.[127]

Clearly the belief that *Samostoyatel'naya Ukraina ne byla i ne budet* (an independent Ukraine has never been and will never be), dies hard among the Russian elite. Similarly, over a decade ago Russia consciously opted for an energy strategy predicted on the idea of forcing Central Asian states to pump gas through the only available pipelines through Russia to Europe at Russian-dictated prices that Moscow could then arbitrage for huge profits rather than develop Russia's own indigenous but hard to develop holdings in eastern Siberia and the Far North. Thus a conscious decision to erect an economic and political structure on the foundation of neo-imperial predation lay at the heart of Russia's economic growth and the enrichment of its elite. Naturally, that elite is loath to forsake "the lure of something exotic in the borderlands."

This contempt for the sovereignty of small states, an abiding Tsarist and Soviet tradition, hardly exhausts the catalogue of other manifestations of the traditionalism of today's Russian state. The public statements of high-ranking foreign ministry and defense officials clearly indicate their open belief that Russia's sovereignty is greater than that of these countries. For example, the 2007 remarks by Chief of Staff General Yuri Baluyevsky that if Poland wants missile defenses, it should also give its people gas masks, reflects the abiding Russian belief that it can bully other states with impunity.[128] Neither are such remarks new tactics in Russian policy. Instead, they have ample precedents going back years. In particular, Russia's ambassadors evidently believe that they have license to interfere in their host countries' domestic politics and make threats indicating their belief in these states' diminished sovereignty, which, of course, in Moscow's eyes make them inferior to Russia whose sovereignty is assumed *a priori* to give it more equality than other states have.

For example, on September 15, 2011, on the eve of the NATO EULEX mission's takeover of the Kosovo customs' points Brnjak and Jarinje, Russian Ambassador Alexander Konuzin created a diplomatic scandal in Serbia that has apparently grown since then. Speaking at the Belgrade Security Forum, Konuzin lambasted the audience and program leaders for not raising questions about this alleged violation of United Nations (UN) Resolution 1244 and other Security Council decisions and asked if there were any Serbs in the audience. Subsequently, he told another Serbian audience in the town of Lazarevac that, while Serbia needs to cooperate with other countries on economic deals, it should not do so to the detriment of Russian-Serbian relations "because that could prove more harmful than useful." Thus he added threats to his earlier screed. Konuzin's impolitic outburst was bad enough, but events since then, including this implicit threat, have only intensified the outcry against Moscow's interference in Serbian domestic affairs and unhappiness with the government's pro-Western policy.

Whatever the merits of the Kosovo issue may be, it appears that this interference is precisely the case. After Konuzin's speech, there was high-profile media coverage of the visit to Russia by leaders of the Serbian Progressive Party (SNS) and Democratic Party of Serbia (DSS) who attended the conference of the ruling United Russia (*Edinaya Rossiya*) party. At this meeting, there was mention of one billion Euros in Russian investments should a "nationally responsible government" be formed. Furthermore, the *Danas* newspaper's collaborators, including former and incumbent government officials in Belgrade outlined what amounts to a network of political officials in the government, Serbian Assembly, various government bodies, and business sectors who advocate on behalf of whatever Moscow's interests are actually very well paid for their work and that this activity has gone on for at least a decade.

Thus Vladimir Beba Popovic, former chief of the Serbian Government's Communications Bureau, told the newspaper, "Russia's role in appointing and dismissing governments in Belgrade was notorious." He also claimed that Russian power centers in the Serbian government and army supported the 2003 assassination of Prime Minister Zoran Djindjic, with the support of agents from the Russian Federal Security Service (FSB). Similarly, Radomir Naumov, Chairman of the Serbian Power Company's Board of Directors and then in 2004 Minister of Energy, was "inspired" by his Russian connections into making dozens of contracts with Russian firms.

Russian TV reporters then interviewed the reporters who broke this story, and they admitted that Konuzin's outburst had inspired them to publish their reporting. But these events clearly ignited a scandal in Serbia. Right wing parties, including the DSS, SNS, and the Serbian Radical Party (SRS) boast of their close ties with analogous organizations in Russia, and there is a lot of smoke, if not fire, suggesting that these organizations are funded by Russia, as well as the fact that some of their leaders have grown rich through business deals with Russia. Naturally, however, these parties deny any and all such charges. [129]

This attitude, reminiscent of the old Brezhnev Doctrine, comes from the top of the government. In particular, it crops up with particular force in regard to the two issues of NATO enlargement and the frozen conflicts in and around the Black Sea littoral. Sergei Markov, Director of the Moscow Institute for political Studies, told a Georgian interviewer in 2006 that, "Georgia has not yet deserved our respect for its sovereignty because it has proved unable to achieve an agreement with the Abkhazian and South Ossetian ethnic minorities."[130] Of course, Markov ignored Russia's unremitting efforts to ensure that conflict resolution cannot take place. So what is one to make of the Russian Ambassador, Vyacheslav Kovalenko's statement that "Russia wants Georgia to be independent, sovereign, and neutral."[131] Since Georgia's political class is united on seeking entry to NATO and then EU, essentially this is a demand that Georgia renounce its independence and leave its territory at risk. Such double talk is not restricted to Georgia. Neither was this an accidental one-time affair. Instead, it represents deeply held views in the Ministry of Foreign Affairs and the government.[132] For instance, as Defense Minister, in 2005 Sergei Ivanov openly updated the Brezhnev Doctrine's concept of diminished sovereignty for Central Asian states, specifically as regards NATO or American bases.

> The countries of the region are members of the Collective Security Treaty Organization (CSTO). And [if the

countries of the region are] making a decision about hosting new bases on their territory, they should take into account the interests of Russia and coordinate this decision with our country.[133]

Ivanov also said that these states should also take preliminary consultations with other members of the Shanghai Cooperation Organization (SCO). This would also give China rights of veto over these states' defense policies and tie them up by obliging them to seek collective permission to conduct an independent defense policy.[134] Echoing this view of the CIS members' inability to stand as fully sovereign independent states, Russian diplomats still cannot fully accept former Soviet republics as genuine states, e.g. diplomats at an Organization for Security Cooperation in Europe (OSCE) meeting calling Georgia "some province."[135] This too represents a deeply held attitude in the Ministry of Foreign Affairs.[136]

The examples of such chauvinism are too many to be accidental. On December 20, 2006, Russia's ambassador to Latvia, Viktor Kaluzhny, made the remarkable statement that:

> The task for Latvia and all other countries is to keep peace therefore they should follow the example of other nations, such as Spain and Italy, which have left Iraq. . . . Latvia, which demands an apology from Russia for Soviet occupation, should apologize to Iraq for participating in its occupation.[137]

This extremely impertinent statement would never have been addressed to Great Britain or Australia, let alone America. But the fact that Kaluzhny, who presumably was authorized to say this, felt free to do so reflects the abiding contempt of Russia's ambassadors for the sovereignty of small European countries, not just the Baltic states. In 1998 Andrei Shvedov, Moscow's Minister Plenipotentiary in Bulgaria, stated that,

> Our position is that NATO's expansion should not be effected to the detriment of any country. No state should be deprived of the right to express its opinion on this matter. Still, the issue remains of whether the entry of a certain state into NATO represents a threat to the security of another country."[138]

Here Moscow sought to dictate to Sofia that it could not have friendly relations with the West and Moscow at the same time, and that Moscow could exercise a veto on its defense and foreign policy. Naturally this gambit went nowhere, and Bulgaria entered NATO at the Istanbul summit in June, 2004.

The failure with Bulgaria did not seem to dissuade Moscow from trying again in even more egregious fashion. Thus in 2002, Russia's new ambassador to Ukraine, former Prime Minister Viktor Chernomyrdin, publicly decried Ukraine's policy of nonalignment with NATO and Russia, calling for a public choice on behalf of Moscow.[139] Chernomyrdin, who clearly acted as if he was sent to be Moscow's proconsul in Kyiv like his Tsarist and Soviet predecessors, has even endorsed candidates in Ukrainian elections since then, and Moscow spent $300 million to manipulate the outcome of the Ukrainian presidential election in 2004, showing again how little actual regard Moscow really has for the sovereignty and independence of Ukraine.

In 2003 Moscow's ambassador to Azerbaijan, Andrei Ryabov, overtook and surpassed his colleagues in the quest for the outstanding chauvinist or neo-colonialist outburst against his hosts. "Provoked" by then U.S. Defense Secretary Donald Rumsfeld's visit to Baku, discussions of U.S. troop deployments there at Azerbaijan's request, and offers by the Pentagon of military assistance to Azerbaijan, Ryabov declared that, "There has not been and there will not be any kind of American presence in the Caspian. We will not allow it, they have nothing to guard here."[140] Ryabov also stated that the appearance of foreign military forces will not ensure, but rather prolong, the conflict in Nagorno-Karabakh, a conflict that has been frozen and where Armenia has hitherto prevailed, not least because of a billion dollars worth of Russian arms transfers to Armenia. Ryabov also argued that "positioning foreign military bases in the territory of other sovereign counties should be considered a partial seizure of those countries' independence." Yet while Ryabov lamented the negative consequences of foreign military bases in an independent country, he conveniently omitted Russia's large military presence in Georgia and Armenia. Nor did he mention the stationing of troops in Moldova.[141]

Finally, at a Hungarian conclave called to celebrate the 50th anniversary of the EU in 2007, opposition leader Viktor Orban, leader of the Hungarian Civic Union (FIDESZ) Party, strongly criticized Russian policies in energy and sharply differentiated between what he called the European and Russian way of thinking. In reply, Moscow's Ambassador to Hungary, Igor Savolsky, took the unusual step of interfering in Hungarian domestic politics and threatened that if Russian businessmen do not feel themselves welcome or secure in the Hungarian market, then they will leave it, i.e., cutting off energy supplies to Hungary.[142]

Thus Russia also still cannot accept the sovereignty of unified states that were former Soviet republics, e.g., Ukraine or Eastern European governments. With that derogation of the present sovereignty of former republics and satellites goes the formulation and implementation of policies designed to undermine it in fact. Self-determination, as was the case under Soviet rule, then becomes a principle to destroy sovereignty. In late 2006, for example, Putin offered Ukraine unsolicited security guarantees in return for permanently stationing the Black Sea Fleet on its territory, a superfluous but ominous gesture inasmuch as Russia had already guaranteed Ukraine's security through the Tashkent treaty of 1992 and the Tripartite agreement with Ukraine and America to denuclearize Ukraine in 1994.[143] Putin's offer also came at the same time as his typically "dialectical" approach to Ukraine's sovereignty in the Crimea where he stated that, "The Crimea forms part of the Ukrainian side and we cannot interfere in another country's internal affairs. At the same time, however, Russia cannot be indifferent to what happens in the Ukraine and Crimea."[144]

In other words, Putin was hinting that Ukrainian resistance to Russian limits on its freedom of action might encounter a Russian backed "Kosovo-like" scenario of a nationalist uprising in the Crimea to which Russia could not remain indifferent. Here we must note that, as one recent commentary puts it:

Moscow has the political and covert action means to create in the Crimea the very type of situations against which Putin is offering to 'protect' Ukraine if the Russian Fleet's presence is extended. Thus far such means have been shown to include inflammatory visits and speeches by Russian Duma deputies in the Crimea, challenges to Ukraine's control of Tuzla Island in the Kerch Strait, the fanning of anti-NATO—in fact anti-American—protests by Russian groups in connection with planned military exercises and artificial Russian-Tatar tensions on the peninsula.[145]

Similarly, in regard to Moldova, Putin in 2000 invoked the Russian diaspora there and other ethnic minorities in an effort to gain more influence over Moldova and its frozen conflict. His justification could have been written by Catherine the Great or, for that matter, Hitler and Stalin.

> Russia is interested in Moldova being a territorially whole, independent state. But this cannot be achieved unless the interests of all population groups, including Transnistria population, are observed. Russia is prepared to participate in creating the conditions in which all residents will feel secure in Moldova. The political treaty must firmly ensure the rights of all those who reside on the territory of Moldova and who consider that Russia can be a guarantor of their rights.[146]

Subsequently, in 2003-04 he sponsored a plan crafted by Dmitri Kozak which was rebuffed by Moldova, leading to perpetual tension between Chisinau and Moscow. An assessment of the Kozak plan observed that its:

> Institutional features were designed to provide Transnistria a veto over any legislation that would threaten the leadership. Ultimately these multiple loci of vetoes would make it impossible for the federal government to operate. In addition, the Kozak Memorandum included clauses that could be interpreted to easily dissolve the federation. For example, the Kozak Memorandum allowed for subjects of the federation to have the right 'to leave the federation in case a decision is taken to unite the federation with another state and (or) in connection with the federation's full loss of sovereignty. . . . [thus] Moldovan integration with international organizations such as the EU could be used as a basis for the dissolution of the federation under this clause'.[147]

It is not suprising that EU and American intervention at the last hour to prevent this outcome apparently enraged Putin and the Kremlin, demonstrating that their idea of partnership with the West, a free hand to reorganize Eurasia, was incompatible with the interests and values of Europe and Washington.[148]

More recently, on October 19, 2011, Turkmenistan's Foreign Ministry blasted Russia's politicized objections to its participation in a Trans-Caspian pipeline (TCP), stating that such a pipeline was an objective vital economic interest of Turkmenistan, rebuked Moscow for "distorting the essence and gist of Turkmenistan's energy policy," and announced that discussions with Europe over this pipeline would continue.[149] Moscow's reply came soon. On November 15, 2011, Valery Yazev, Vice-Speaker of the Russian Duma and head of the Russian Gas Society, openly threatened Turkmenistan with the Russian incitement of an "Arab Spring" if it did not renounce its "neutrality" and independent sovereign foreign policy, including its desire to align with Nabucco. Yazev said that:

> Given the instructive experience with UN resolutions on Libya and the political consequences of their being 'shielded from the air' by NATO forces, Turkmenistan will soon understand that only the principled positions of Russia and China in the UN Security Council and its involvement in regional international organizations — such as the SCO (Shanghai Cooperation Organization), CSTO (Collective Security Treaty Organization), Eurasian Economic Union — can protect it from similar resolutions.[150]

In other words, Turkmenistan should surrender its neutrality and independent foreign policy and not ship gas to Europe; otherwise, Moscow will incite a revolution there leading to chaos. Other Russian analysts and officials threatened that if Turkmenistan adheres to the EU's planned Southern Corridor for energy transshipments to Europe that bypass Russia, Moscow would have no choice but to do to Turkmenistan what it did to Georgia in 2008.[151]

Russian observers fully understand the intrinsically imperial or neo-imperial cognitive foundation of this great power mantra. For instance, Alexei Malashenko observed that Russia's response to the Chechen threat in 1999-2000 only made sense if Russia continues to regard itself as an empire.[152] Since then, Russian political scientist Egor Kholmogorov has observed that:

> 'Empire' is the main category of any strategic political analysis in the Russian language. Whenever we start to ponder a full-scale, long-term construction of the Russian state, we begin to think of empire and in terms of empire. Russians are inherently imperialists.[153]

If Russia is an empire of this sort or still hankers for that empire, then it becomes clear why membership in NATO or the EU of former Soviet republics or even of Russia's erstwhile satellites in Eastern Europe becomes a threat to Russian sovereignty and why Russia must be an independent sovereign actor, unbounded by any other political association and exercising unfettered power in its own domain. Moreover, it is essential for the concept of Derzhavnost' (i.e., Russia as a unique, autocratic, great power) not only that Russia assert its great power status but that it be recognized as such by other states and thus granted a superior status, first of all, vis-à-vis the neighboring CIS countries. Thus in its 1999 official submission to the EU of its strategy for relations with that organization, made by then Prime Minister Vladimir Putin, the Russian government stated that:

> As a world power situated on two continents, Russia should retain its freedom to determine and implement its foreign and domestic policies, its status and advantages of a Euro-Asian state and largest country of the CIS. The "development of partnership with the EU should contribute to consolidating Russia's role as the leading power in shaping a new system of interstate political and economic relations in the CIS area." and thus, Russia would "oppose any attempts to hamper economic integration in the CIS [that may be made by the EU], including through 'special relations' with individual CIS member states to the detriment of Russia's interests."[154]

The concurrent and deep-rooted demand for recognition of Russia as a great power with a right to an exclusive sphere of influence in the former Soviet Union and a global great power status originated with Yeltsin at exactly the same time as the drift towards autocracy and the end of reforms began, i.e., in 1992-93. Indeed, these beliefs in Russia's intrinsic great powerness and the demand for a sphere of influence in the CIS are linked, for in the minds of many of this elite if Russia is not a great power, i.e., a neo-imperial empire, it will not only not be a great power, it will be anything other than a newly minted version of medieval appendage princedoms. Moreover, as many analysts claim, democracy is contraindicated to the preservation of the large state, if not the state as such, because it will lead to Islamist rule in the south and other similar breakdowns of power at the center.[155]

In a recent publication of a U.S.-Russian dialogue, Russian participants made their views clear.

Russian participants in dialogue meetings argued that Russia's principal objective in the former Soviet region was to strengthen the country's security by ensuring that governments there remained stable and friendly. From Moscow's perspective, American democracy promotion is a direct threat because it disrupts the existing political order — introducing instability — and, because of Washington's selectivity and varied standards, appears to be aimed primarily at installing pro-American governments rather than democratic ones. This dynamic drove much of the U.S.-Russian discussion and interaction in Central Asia during the Bush Administration.[156]

However, this perspective only tells part of the story. In fact, as can be seen from Moscow's response to the Arab revolutions of 2011, democracy is the greatest enemy of the state. Since Russia is obviously not interested in truly improving the security of former Soviet allies or republics, but in dominating them for its own unilateral advantage, it is unwilling to give up their freedom of action in world politics. As a result, Moscow regards democracy as such as a threat and, like its Tsarist and Soviet predecessors, has internalized the Leninist threat paradigm that reformers at home are paid agents of foreign influence. Therefore, as Sergei Ivanov, then Defense Minister and Deputy Prime Minister, wrote in 2006, suggesting that the main threat to Russia is democracy as such, i.e., a democratic revolution in Russia or a neighboring CIS state, not an invasion by any foreign regime or terorrists.[157] Democracy and revolution, or autonomous public political action beyond the limits imposed by the state is generally, if not always, the result of a conspiracy from abroad. Thus the media and the government regularly denounce U.S. initiatives to distribute cellular technology or use the Internet, or the Internet itself as part of a conspiracy from abroad, and their first response to such crises is (and this is typical of all authoritarian regimes), of course, to shut down, or at least restrict the use of information and social technologies and networks.[158]

In keeping with the inherited Soviet and KGB mentality and the traditions of projection onto the enemy of your own fears and intentions that was so prominent in Stalin's makeup, they regularly assert that such revolutions are therefore merely the product of external manipulation and subversion, overlooking the domestic roots of such upheavals. Thus it is now the case in professional Russian military writing that the term "color revolution" is now described essentially as a revolution stage-managed from outside by external political actors with an interest in the constitution of power in the affected state. The citizens of that state are merely passive bystanders or puppets of this external manifestation, a clear projection outward of how the Russian government views or wants to view its own citizens, and also the threats to it from their arousal.[159]

Similarly President Medvedev could say, with regard to the Arab revolutions of 2011:

> Look at the current situation in the Middle East and the Arab world. It is extremely difficult and great problems still lie ahead. In some cases it may even come to the disintegration of large, heavily populated states, their break-up into smaller fragments. The character of these states is far from straightforward. It may come to very complex events, including the arrival of fanatics into power. This will mean decades of fires and further spread of extremism. We must face the truth. In the past such a scenario was harbored for us, and now

attempts to implement it are even more likely. In any case, this plot will not work. But everything that happens there will have a direct impact on our domestic situation in the long term, as long as decades.[160]

Neither is it surprising that Putin *et al.*, continue to raise the phobia of Western instigation as a pretext for intervention and plots against Russia.[161]

Therefore a unitary state, led by an autocrat is not only a domestic necessity; it also is a foreign policy necessity as what a contemporary great power means, if not a full-fledged empire. This view dates back to the Bolsheviks, if not the Tsars. For example, Stalin in 1920 wrote about the Soviet borderlands that:

> Only two alternatives confront the border regions: Either they join forces with Russia and then the toiling masses of the border regions will be emancipated from imperialist oppression; or they join forces with the Entente, and then the yoke of imperialism is inevitable.[162]

Indeed, Moscow has historically feared reform and democracy originating in the borderlands and peripheries of its empire. For example, Ukraine's historic role as a gateway for Western ideas into Russia makes a reformed, democratic, stable, and secure Ukraine enormously important for European security.[163] Ukraine tied to Russia allows Moscow to restore its imperial role and threaten Europe. Contrarily, without empire a Russian autocracy is much harder to sustain. Consequently, Russia has no choice but to conjure phony threat scenarios, subvert neighboring regimes and European states, and intimidate everyone.

Western power, embodied in these treaties and organizations like the OSCE, translates into an often resented pressure upon neighboring states to democratize their economic-military-state organizations in ways that challenge Russia's system and imperial pretenses. Those reformed organizations could become more effective comparative models for their political, economic, and military organization. As we know from Tsarist and Soviet times, the demonstration effect of trends from Central and Eastern Europe into the former Soviet Union, Russia, and now into Central Asia generally generates pressures for modernization that corrode existing anti-democratic regimes.[164] Similarly in Russian foreign policy, anti-reformers triumphed with regard to Asian policy so that by 1993 authoritarian China, not democratic Japan, was regarded as Moscow's principal partner in Asia, not least because of its anti-reform and anti-American proclivities.[165]

While many Russian elites view this Western pressure as a conspiracy and threat to Russia's integrity and state, they have no viable answer to this challenge.[166] The Paris Peace Treaty of 1990 and the OSCE's 1991 Moscow Declaration, foundation documents of today's world order, state that democratic norms and their observation by the states parties to those agreements are "matters of direct and legitimate concern to all participating States and do not belong exclusively to the internal affairs of the state concerned."[167] Thus their laws and their legal, military, and political institutions derive their legitimacy from these documents, and Russia's regressive state system duly risks being branded as illegitimate, not just ineffectual.[168] Those treaties are the product of the George H. W. Bush administration that was singularly deficient in the "vision thing." Yet they provide legal force to the idea that domestic sovereignty can be challenged politically by foreign governments and actors, and that states have a legitimate right to place other states' domestic

93

political conduct under an international microscope and even to intervene if necessary to prevent unacceptable domestic conduct.[169]

This Derzhavnost' outlook also clearly influences and lies behind recent efforts to generate an ideology of "sovereign democracy" for Russia to depict its status and place in the world as a state enjoying a uniquely independent standing unlike most other states. This notion of both intrinsic and threatened great power status that must therefore be fought for every day thus ties together other deeply felt and long-standing Russian concepts, the belief in its uniqueness, the supposed refusal to accept the standards and limits placed upon other states, and its untrammeled sovereignty, pertaining to both that of the autocrat at home and of the Russian state abroad. Therefore, Russia must be not only an empire but also a wholly freestanding actor in world politics. Moreover, by virtue of its assumed status and implicit (if not actual) capabilities, Russia, as people like Foreign Minister Sergei Lavrov say, should be a system-forming power in today's world politics, not just the CIS.[170]

Policymakers also stated these views and ambitions at the dawn of Putin's presidency. For as Deputy Foreign Minister Ivan Ivanov stated in 1999:

> Our country is not in need of affiliation with the EU. This would entail loss of its unique Euro-Asian specifics, the role of the center of attraction of the re-integration of the CIS, independence in foreign economic and defense policies, and complete restructuring (once more) of all Russian statehood based on the requirements of the European Union. Finally great powers (and it is too soon to abandon calling ourselves such) do not dissolve in international unions — they create them around themselves.[171]

So while Russian history may have bequeathed a heavy imperial legacy, Russian state policy, the current nature of the state, and its resemblance to earlier formations to a significant degree represent the result of conscious elite decisions to seize power and hold it in accordance with Russian traditions, i.e., without recourse to democratic and legal means, even if today's world is utterly transformed from that of the past. Those traditions most assuredly include as a key core interest of the state the retention of its neo-imperial outlook, tendencies, and powers.

That too is not an accidental or arbitrary coincidence with the turn towards autocracy at home and neo-imperialism abroad. In the chaos of that time, the armed forces usurped foreign policy to carry out interventions in Moldova and Georgia that set the stage for a neo-imperial reassertion of Russia and the persisting frozen conflicts that have remained unresolved since then. Troops occupied the Transdniester, supported rebels against Georgia in South Ossetia and Abkhazia, and Russia shipped $1 billion of weapons to Armenia in its campaign in Nagorno-Karabakh against Azerbaijan. It is no accident that these were the states that most defiantly asserted their right not to remain tied to Russia. By 1993, Yeltsin was publicly advocating this sphere of influence and giving every sign of autocratic power seeking. So it is also hardly a coincidence that states in Eastern Europe: Poland, Hungary, and the Czech and Slovak Republics, all began to assert their interest in joining NATO at this time. While U.S. policy was and is hardly irreproachable, it does not bear sole, or maybe even primary responsibility for the decline in relations with Russia. Russia may like to portray itself as the victim (and has habitually done so) of misguided or treacherous Western policies. But objective analysts cannot let Russia off the hook of its own responsibility so easily.

RUSSIAN FOREIGN POLICY AND RUSSIAN HISTORY

As we noted, Rieber's search for persistent challenges to Russian foreign policymakers originated in dissatisfaction with the pieties of Russian historiography that this author shares. Few, if any, studies of Russian foreign policy since 1991 have taken Russian history before Mikhail Gorbachev's valiant but doomed effort to reform the Soviet Union into account.[172] Equally disquieting is the fact that far too many contemporary discussions of Russian foreign policy implicitly assume that foreign policy in Russia and the issues confronting Moscow only began with Gorbachev. Earlier Sovietological accounts made the same mistake, assuming that foreign policy issues only began under Brezhnev, Nikita Khrushchev, or Stalin, etc. Obviously, this is not the case, and Vladimir Putin did not happen upon a foreign policy landscape that was only created or fell from the sky in the 1990s.

These accounts often share the same flaws. They begin with Gorbachev and forget about the period preceding him. Second, virtually every study of post-Soviet foreign policy divides Russian foreign policy practitioners and analysts in Russia into three camps. Whatever title one ascribes to these groups, we usually come down with an approach that finds conservatives, moderates, and liberals whose views are most often analyzed without any reference to Russian domestic or contemporary international politics, let alone Russian history. While foreign policy ideas may be free floating, they do not originate in the stratosphere and then descend to earth. Rather, they originate as a response to concrete political and economic situations. Given the inherent fluidity and dynamism of contemporary politics, these situations often seem to be new and unexpected to policymakers or unlike earlier issues even when there are connections to the past. Nonetheless, we, unlike politicians, may draw analytical connections to past experiences and issues that provide useful insight into a country's foreign policy.

Those continuities in Russian history include, *inter alia*,

- The long chronicle of colonization and conquest; Russia's historic attractiveness to other elites in neighboring countries that made up for the empire building phase of Russian history through 1945, if not 1991 when the Union of Soviet Socialist Republics (USSR) collapsed.
- Russia's "longevity" as an imperial great power dating back to Peter the Great, if not earlier, while other contenders fell out of the competition; the enduring longevity of Russian statesmen's belief that Russia is or should be seen as an empire or great power regardless of the facts of the case at any given time.
- The presence of its frontier of weakly consolidated states that offered numerous opportunities for subversion and then annexation and incorporation of adding territories, and the concentration of political power and hence of foreign policymaking in the hands of a small group of people clustered around one ruler.[173]
- Other enduring geopolitical considerations are the regime's abiding awareness that other states

with which Russia must interact are ahead of it in economics, democracy, technology cultural sophistication as defined by Western canons and often military power.

In that connection, we might also cite the long-standing perception by Russian elites that Russia is not truly seen by Europe as a fully European and legitimate state either politically or culturally, a stance that obliges Russia to fight constantly for recognition and to be taken seriously.[174] But at the same time, the unlimited claims made on behalf of Russia by its leaders and diplomats reflects their perception of dealing with treacherous and often superior foreigners by whose standards (and those became standards by which Russia wanted to present itself after Peter the Great) Russia was increasingly seen as a barbarous, illegitimate, and threatening tyranny. Indeed, virtually from the outset of its history as a state, Russia has suffered from the European and now possibly global perspective that while it commands great power and material resources, it is not truly a great power because it remains in some crucial sense an uncivilized, rude, and barbarous kingdom that does not accept the true European or Western, or global standard of what statehood and its responsibilities now means.[175] Consequently, much of the history of Russian diplomacy from its inception until the present is Russia's determined and obsessive quest for status as it sees itself, and an effort to make others see Russia and accept it as the Russian government wants to see itself and be seen by others. If it is not so perceived, Russia will sulk, seek vengeance, and continue to make trouble until it is taken seriously.

This demand for taking Russia seriously lies at the heart of the issue in East-West relations because Moscow believes and has complained that the West as a whole, and particularly America, does not take it or its interests sufficiently seriously, i.e., at Moscow's own, but often self-serving, and inflated valuation of itself. Putin's presidential envoy for relations with the EU, Sergei Yastrzhembskiy, stated that this was Russia's main objection to recent developments in world politics.[176] Similarly, Russia's Ambassador to America, Yuri Ushakov wrote in 2007 that:

> What offends us is the view shared by some in Washington that Russia can be used when it is needed and discarded or even abused when it is not relevant to American objectives. . . . Russians do not need any special favors or assistance from the United States, but we do require respect in order to build a two-way relationship. And we expect that our political interests will be recognized.[177]

Similarly, in 2007 then Deputy Prime Minister Dmitry Medvedev told the annual Davos Conference that while nobody was obliged to love Russia, it would demand the respect that it deserves. Later that year, he asserted that through its own efforts, Russia had returned to the great power status that it deserved and would not tolerate being told off like a naughty pupil.[178] Since then, for example in 2009 and endlessly since then, Moscow has repeatedly said:

> The further development of our partnership with the alliance will depend in a large part on whether NATO is prepared to maintain a dialogue on a fair and equal basis, with mutual interests and concerns taken into account and to build relations with Russia in the security area not as with an opponent but as a partner.[179]

Unfortunately, those terms mean that NATO gives Russia a veto on its activities, while Russia has near complete freedom of action in its sphere of influence, and that its domestic policies, unlike those of the West, remain free from any external criticism or rebuke. Obviously, neither the United States, nor NATO, nor any European state, nor the CIS states can freely accept such an abridgement of its or their independence and sovereignty along with the unraveling of the post-1991 status quo in Europe. This is where the issue is and will be joined for a long time to come. As Sergei Markedonov wrote in 2009:

> Russia has its regional interests, resources to defend them, and a legitimate motivation to protect them. Acknowledging these interests could basically make the process of "resetting" indeed something meaningful. However, for this NATO (and its main engine), the United States need to seriously change their assessments of post-Soviet realities, and Russia needs to substantially moderate its global ambitions (especially when it is impossible to pay for them).[180]

But since the reset of the policy of 2009, Europe and the United States have indeed moved in the direction specified by Markedonov. But Moscow has not done so and, indeed, the nature of its political system precludes such movement. Thus, we can behold the continuing crisis of bipolarity in Europe and Eurasia.

- Culturally, the abiding and insoluble issue of defining a national identity adequate to Russia's state continues as both intellectuals and policymakers cannot make up their minds as to whether Russia is a European state, a bridge between Europe and Asia, a uniquely Eurasian phenomenon, a national state or a multinational empire or both, or all of the above, etc.

- Finally, and most consistently, is the long struggle by Russian Tsars and subsequent leaders to ensure the continuity of the autocratic patrimonial state in its various guises and to defend it not only physically but increasingly intellectually against Western onslaughts. This is a domain where we can most visibly see the continuity in historical thinking among the elite. This particular task has been a challenge at least since Catherine the Great's time, if not since the state's inception under Ivan III, and it continues to this day. The following examples underscore this continuity. The famous justification for Tsarist rule was the immaturity, backwardness, etc., of the Russian people, and this was summed up in the Russian word *Popechitel'stvo*, (tutelage). But the Bolsheviks took it up soon after they seized power. In 1918, Bolshevik Commissar of Enlightenment, Anatoly Lunacharsky, justified the Bolshevik dictatorship in words that could have come out of the mouth of any Tsarist official after Peter the Great. Namely, he said that the masses' ignorance precluded their self-government whose precondition was their own enlightenment.[181] Lenin's whole approach grew out of his conviction that the working class could not of its own accord liberate itself. Since that had not happened, Soviet power had to rule by what Lunacharsky termed "enlightened absolutism." Because the old intelligentsia opposed Bolshevism, Lunacharsky argued that "we, the avant-garde, must have the power since we represent the correct understanding of the majority's interest. Power must therefore reside in the proletarian dictatorship."[182]

More recently, Deputy Prime Minister and then Defense Minister Sergei Ivanov replied to a question about the concept of "Kremlin Inc.," in the following manner. (It should be noted that the elite speak of the system as a corporation, so this was not an innocent question.)

> It's just a nice phrase, a journalistic turn of phrase. But I would say that you need to understand our history, our mentality. Russia is a huge country and mentally, unfortunately the majority of the population, as before, relies on the Tsar. Our civil society is weak. It can't be strong because only 15 years have passed since it began to be created. Before then, you'll agree there was not the slightest condition for it to be created. It is still very young. Therefore, you can't see questions of concentration of management in Russia only through the prism of Anglo-Saxon political culture. Russia will never take its model of management completely, 100 percent from that Anglo-Saxon political elite. Whether you like it or not is a different question, but I am telling you how it is.[183]

In the same interview, Ivanov called democracy a *bardak*, i.e., a particularly slovenly brothel.[79] Here Ivanov self-consciously invoked the Russian autocratic tradition as justification to prove our point.

Similarly, Putin and Medvedev have both made it clear that they will never let Russia be governed as is Ukraine where there is a much greater pluralistic or democratic component.[184] But this refusal to alter the autocratic nature of the state, even if reform from the top is contemplated, means that the state is also increasingly aware throughout modern times that its legitimacy is suspect and that its people's desire for autonomous political self-expression is deeply to be feared. Furthermore, its rhetoric of being a besieged fortress and the enduring argument that reformers at home are enemies linked with Western governments and intelligence agencies ensures the continuation of the Leninist threat paradigm linking both sets of enemies together and freezing the regime in an *a priori* hostility towards the West. Neither is it surprising that Putin *et al.*, continue to raise the phobia of Western instigation as a pretext for intervention and plots against Russia.[185] Cynics may say this is just for domestic consumption, but it clearly reflects leaders' anxieties while simultaneously creating a corresponding domestic demand for autocratic and strongman rule.

The flip side of this defense against democracy is the postulation of Russian statehood in terms that clearly evoke conservative and Slavophile (if not still more reactionary) platitudes developed since the 17th century, if not even earlier. For Dmitri Trenin, Russia is "authoritarianism with the consent of the governed," i.e., an exact restatement of a Slavophile ideal that itself looks backward to the medieval Zemsky Sobor (Council of the Land).[186] The renowned movie director, Nikita Mikhalkov, has praised the "conservatism" of Russian culture and the Russian mind that unites "ecclesiastic, monarchist, Soviet, and liberal ideologies." Democracy is contrary to Russian tradition and incompatible with Russia's size, therefore the current regime is indispensable.[187] These ideas are no more original than is Trenin's description of the state though Trenin is much more accurate. The examples of this invocation of a mystical Russian history to justify the regime are omnipresent.

Chairman of the State Duma Boris Gryzlov professes that "autocratic people power" (*Samoderzhvnoye*

Narodovlastiye) is the same thing as sovereign democracy and is uniquely indigenous and historically characteristic of Russia. By making this proclamation, Gryzlov also consciously invokes the history of the idea of the Zemsky Sobor, and the Slavophile notion of *Sobornost'* ("conciliarity") in order to justify a picture that looks remarkably like an expanded version of the medieval Boyar Duma, namely the Prince and his retinue of nobles, as the rulers of Russia. Thus history and the use of history as justifications for power at home and abroad continue to shape Russian foreign policy.

Indeed, Gryzlov, like innumerable publicists before him in Russian history, argues that Russian democracy (much to most observers' amazement) is characterized by collaboration and harmony between the executive and legislative powers.[188] This kind of reasoning implicitly rejects the need to have a separation of powers and is a hallmark of Russian autocracy and political thought. Given the near total emasculation of the legislature in today's Russia; such reasoning strikes us as Orwellian, if not preposterous. But undoubtedly it expresses the thinking and cynicism of Russian leaders. Medvedev, in his 2008 campaign, expressly stated the presidential system represents the Russian historical tradition, and with any other system Russia would fall apart.[189] This idea, that without autocracy Russia would fall apart and count for nothing in world politics, dates back at least to the 18th century, if not earlier, and is a cornerstone of Russian conservative thinking, to the suppression of all thought of reform.[190]

As Ivanov's interview showed, Russians, especially the current elite, insist on Russia's specificity, most particularly with regard to the nature of the political order and regime, whereas Westerners continue to insist on seeing it in terms of the categories of Western political thought.[191] Indeed, official commentaries invoke the nature of Russian history as proof of this uniqueness and thus of the justification of the present order.[192] A recent speech by President Medvedev makes clear the deliberately politicized and mythologized history of the state that the Kremlin today (tomorrow, as we know, it may change) wants to present. Unfortunately, little or none of it is true. Thus Medvedev said that:

> Russian statehood initially developed on a multiethnic basis and did not follow a path of division, but rather, a path of unification. And that is the only reason why today we have such a unique nation. Even then, fragmentation was seen as a factor of weakness, and in the process of creating the nation, there were no significant barriers to cultural and religious diversity, which, again, allowed for the creation of such a unique state as the Russian Empire, and subsequently, the Russian Federation. I feel that this is one of the truly serious, genuinely fundamental lessons in history. Moreover, consolidation into one state also promoted the emergence of common values. These common values served as the foundation for developing new norms of social life and common rules of behavior, as well as the development of relations with European and subsequently Asian nations. And, of course, people adopted the leading examples of culture and modern ideas of the time. There is another fact that has to do with the law, which is of particular interest to me as a member of the legal community. We have discussed it with historians. Initially, Russia was formed as a law-governed state, that is, as a state with its own rules of conduct that in modern terms we refer to as laws. These rules of conduct regulated relationships between people, maintained public order, and, therefore, sustained a certain lifestyle and values. This

idea of a law-governed Russian state at that time was part of the general idea of justice: the government is needed so that the state can develop and people will live better, and so the government should take into account both the interests of ordinary people and their traditions, the traditions of different peoples who live together in a large country.[193]

Indeed, Medvedev explicitly stated that the reason for propounding this theory are explicitly political, i.e., justifying his political project, and nationalistic in terms of the state. Thus:

Why do I say this? Because there are all kinds of negativist notions, denying the legal nature of the Russian state, showing a lack of respect for our legal traditions, the sense that we are inferior in some way up to the point that statehood came to Russia from somewhere in Western Europe, whereas we were not able to come up with it ourselves. We all realize that this is completely wrong, of course, but at the same time it is very damaging. That's why I think that the discussion about the legal nature of the Russian state also has value in itself. If it is a law-governed state, fundamentally based on the law, even with all its defects, then such a state can develop along the democratic path, which is our goal today. Otherwise, the conclusion would have to be different, and that would set us back 100 years.[194]

Thus Medvedev's speech, like innumerable citations from leaders before him, once again invokes the centuries-old tradition of the state determining for political purposes what Russian history is, and second, defending that history as a purely autochthonic process in ways calculated to belittle foreign influence on Russia's development and appeal to Russia's unique state nationalism. This official mythmaking appeals to deeply rooted and obviously cherished concepts of

Russian culture even if they have little grounding in the actual historical truth. If we may paraphrase the cynical view expressed at the conclusion of the film, "The Man Who Shot Liberty Valance," when the truth contradicts the legend, "Print the legend."

Furthermore, since its birth as a state during the reign of Ivan III or Ivan the Great, 1462-1505, Russia and its leaders have continually stressed the uniqueness and special, even sacred character of Russia that distinguishes it from all other governments or states. As Ivanov demonstrated, this perspective still dominates the ruling class. Indeed, as Russian commentators know this hostility towards the West and democracy is almost obsessive. For example, Vladimir Shlapentokh has shown that an essential component of the Kremlin's ideological campaign to maintain the Putin regime in power and extend it past the elections of 2008 is anti-Americanism. Thus:

> The core of the Kremlin's ideological strategy is to convince the public that any revolution in Russia will be sponsored by the United States. Putin is presented as a bulwark of Russian patriotism, as the single leader able to confront America's intervention in Russian domestic life and protect what is left of the imperial heritage. This propaganda is addressed mostly to the elites (particularly elites in the military and FSB) who sizzle with hatred and envy of America.[195]

Similarly Russia has accepted a threat perception, for which ultimately there is no solution for as the Russian philosopher Sergei Gavrov writes:

> The threats are utopian, the probability of their implementation is negligible, but their emergence is a sign.

This sign—a message to "the city and the world"—surely lends itself to decoding and interpretation: we will defend from Western claims our ancient right to use our imperial (authoritarian and totalitarian) domestic socio-cultural traditions within which power does not exist to serve people but people exist to serve power.[196]

These are not isolated views either. Russian journalist Leonid Radzikhovsky has said, "The existential void of our politics has been filled entirely by anti-Americanism" and that to renounce this rhetoric "would be tantamount to destroying the foundations of the state ideology."[197] Similarly, Fedor Lukyanov, Editor of *Russia in Global Affairs*, writes that:

The mentality of Russian politics is such that relations with the United States remain at the center of universal attention and virtually any problems are seen though an American prism. This is partially a reflection of inertia of thinking which is finding it hard to break with perceptions of Cold War times. It is partially a demonstration of a hidden desire to have a sense of our own significance. There is still a desire to compare ourselves specifically with the only superpower.[198]

Lukyanov also notes that both the United States and Russia see the other as being a power in decline.[199] At least one Russian writer boasts that Russia bears primary responsibility for frustrating American unilateralism by shaping blocking coalitions that restrained and ultimately foiled U.S. designs.[200] This kind of thinking would conform to the contention by Kari Roberts, a Canadian scholar, that, "It appears as though the common themes in Russian foreign policymaking continue to be how Russia views itself vis-à-vis the United States and its pragmatic approach to identifying and tackling foreign policy problems."[201] For example, there is good reason to see Russia's Iranian policy as being closely tied to its perceptions of U.S. policies.

For an understanding of security policy, we must emphasize that the intrinsic nature of this autocratic service state condemns it to constant suspicion of all its neighbors and to their equal distrust of Russian objectives. This state's abiding sense of insecurity is, first of all, domestic. Its leaders' habitual resort to fraud, corruption, and electoral manipulation, if not to violence, against critics, bespeaks its leaders' inner awareness of the fragility of their rule, the short-term time horizons of the elite that never knows when everything might be taken away from them, and the illegitimacy of their power. The determination to preserve the autocratic matrix intact as far as possible sets the stage for a state in permanent crisis against its own people because of the ever-present danger of revolution. The vast armies and police forces (multiple incarnations of each as well) that typified Tsarist and Soviet rule still characterize contemporary Russia, and it is increasingly clear that they are deployed to prevent the public from asserting its civic, human, and political rights, thereby creating the ever-present potential for a civil war with inherently international implications.

There is ample evidence that both these dangers of unrest or of heightened forcible repression are growing, along with the authorities' perception of the manifestation of popular unrest due to the current economic crisis.[202] Already in 2005-06, the Ministry of Defense (MOD) formed Special Designation Forces from Spetsnaz brigades under the Minister's direct control. They have air, marine, and ground components and conduct peace support and counterterrorist operations.[203] Since the minister answers only to the president, essentially this also means putting all Russia under threat of counterterrorist or other so called operations without any Parliamentary accountability or scrutiny.

Since then, matters have, if anything, grown worse. An April 2009 report outlined quite clearly the threat perceived by the authorities. Specifically, it stated that:

> The Russian intelligence community is seriously worried about latent social processes capable of leading to the beginning of civil wars and conflicts on RF territory that can end up in a disruption of territorial integrity and the appearance of a large number of new sovereign powers. Data of an information "leak," the statistics and massive number of antigovernment actions, and official statements and appeals of the opposition attest to this.[204]

This report proceeded to say that these agencies expected massive protests in the Moscow area, industrial areas of the South Urals and Western Siberia and in the Far East while ethnic tension among the Muslims of the North Caucasus and Volga-Ural areas is also not excluded. The author also invoked the specter of enraged former Army officers and soldiers who are now being demobilized because of the reforms that should dramatically reduce the armed forces might also take to the streets with their weapons. But while this unrest threatened, the government is characteristically resorting to strong-arm methods to meet this threat. In other words, it is repeating past regimes (not the least Yeltsin's) in strengthening the Internal Troops of the Ministry of Internal Affairs (VVMVD) and now other paramilitary forces as well.[205]

More soberly, this report, along with other articles, outlines the ways in which the internal armed forces are being strengthened. Special intelligence and commando subunits to conduct preventive elimination of opposition leaders are being established in the VVMVD. These forces are also receiving new models of weapons and equipment, armored, artillery, naval, and air defense systems. In 2008, 5.5 Billion rubles was allocated for these forces' modernization. Apart from the already permitted "corporate forces" of Gazprom and Transneft that monitor pipeline safety, the Ministry of Internal Affairs (MVD) is also now discussing an *Olimpstroi* (Olympics Construction) Army, and even the Fisheries inspectorate is going to create a special armed subunit called Piranha.[206]

Since then, even more information about the extent of the domestic reconstruction of the MVD into a force intended to suppress any manifestation of dissent have emerged. As of 2003, there were 98 special-purpose police detachments (OMONs) in Russia. By comparison, in 1988 during the crisis of the regime and its elites under Gorbachev, 19 OMONs were created in 14 Russian regions and three union republics. By 2007, there were already 121 OMON units comprising 20,000 men operating in Russia. Moreover, by 2007 there were another 87 police special designation detachments (OMSNs) with permanent staffing of over 5,200 people operating with the internal affairs organs, making a grand total of 208 special purpose or designated units with 25,000 well-trained and drilled soldiers. The OMSNs have grown from an anti-crime and anti-terrorist force to a force charged with stopping extremist criminal activity. All these units train together and have been centralized within the MVD to fight organized crime, terrorism, and extremism. From 2005 to 2006, the financing of these units was almost doubled. By 2009, they were also working with aircraft assets, specifically the MVD's own Aviation Center with nine special purpose air detachments throughout Russia. Seven more such units are to be created.

Furthermore, the MVD has developed a concept for rapidly airlifting these forces to troubled areas from other regions when necessary. These forces are also receiving large-scale deliveries of new armored vehicles with computers in some cases and command, control, communications (C3) capabilities. Since these are forces apart from the regular VVMVD, "On a parallel basis with the OMON empire, a multi-level internal security troop machine is being developed with its own special forces, aircraft, armored equipment, situational-crisis centers, and so forth."[207] When one considers this huge expansion of the domestic *Silovye Struktury*, it becomes clear why already in 2008 Russia announced that it would increase funding for the Ministry of Interior by 50 percent in 2010, and where the government's estimation of the true threat to Russian security lies.[208]

The striking continuity of elite thinking and policy over several centuries should not come as a surprise to students of Russia. But what it does show, beyond the continuing relevance of Russian history, is the degree of elite consensus that had been attained by the time Putin came to power. Beyond that, Ivanov's remarks show just how much the elite invokes Russian history as a justification for its rule and how much it insists upon Russia's specificity (*spetsifichnost'*) as part of that justification. Indeed, such invocations are themselves long-standing phenomena of Russian history. Unfortunately, as shown above, today's state is very much a product of and bears a strong resemblance to what preceded it. Yet, precisely because these issues never have been and probably cannot be conclusively resolved, they continue to haunt the minds of policy-makers, analysts, and foreign observers of Russian foreign policy.

Second, as Ivanov's words above indicate, the leaders' sense of constant insecurity is a permanent feature of its foreign policy. This is not just the iden-tification of democracy as the enemy or of the linkage between domestic reformers and external powers. It also relates to the struggle over the borderlands as re-flected in Stalin's statement above and the consistent policy aiming to subvert the new states' sovereignty. Russia's contemporary leadership, like the Bolsheviks, sees itself in a state of siege with both democracy and other great powers. How else can we explain the vast increase in Russian intelligence operations against the United States, its allies, and Russia's neighbors under Putin?

The continuation of geopolitical conflict, much to the chagrin of many U.S. intellectuals who think it should have ended with the end of the Cold War, is not the same thing as the Cold War. In any case, accord-ing to prominent and well-connected Russian experts like Sergei Karaganov, the Cold War never ended and still goes on. Karaganov, director of the semi-official Council on Foreign and Defense Policy, wrote in the *Jordan Times* in 2009 that not only had the Cold War not ended, it never really finished.

> NATO, moreover, not only enlarged its membership, but also transformed itself from an anti-communist defensive alliance into an offensive grouping (with operations in Yugoslavia, Iraq and Afghanistan). NA-TO's expansion towards Russia's own borders, and the membership of countries whose elites have his-torical complexes in regard to Russia, increased anti-

Russian sentiment inside the alliance. For all its efforts to improve its image, many Russians now view NATO as a much more hostile organization than they did in the 1990s, or even before then. Moreover, NATO enlargement has meant that Europe itself has still not emerged from the cold war. No peace treaty ended the cold war, so it remains unfinished. Even though the ideological and military confrontation of those times is far behind us, it is being replaced with a new standoff - between Russia, on one hand, and the U.S. and some of the "New Europeans" on the other. My hope is that, when historians look back at Georgia's attack on South Ossetia of last summer, the Ossetians, Russians, and Georgians killed in that war will be seen as having not died in vain. Russian troops crushed Georgia's army on the ground, but they also delivered a strong blow against the logic of further NATO expansion, which, if not stopped, would have inevitably incited a major war in the heart of Europe.[209]

Lest we think that the U.S. reset policy towards Russia has altered this point of view, we should consider the following evidence. Dmitri Trenin recently wrote that:

> The opinion that has predominated in our country to this day that the 'reset' is above all Washington's apology for the mistakes of the earlier Bush Administration and their rectification certainly does not correspond to the idea of the current team in the White House. For example, in our country the concept of the 'reset' is understood as almost the willingness in current conditions to accept the Russian point of view of the situation in the Near Abroad, which essentially is wishful thinking.[210]

Similarly, Russia's Ambassador to NATO, Dmitri Rogozin, said in March 2009, "any new relationship with NATO would be on Moscow's terms."[211]

THE QUEST FOR SECURITY

Precisely because of this backwardness of the state, society, and economy and this uncertainty as to whether Russia belongs to some specific community of states and has the means to participate in its international interactions, it has been a constant effort for Russia to import the resources necessary for effective political competition from the very states that it regards as rivals, if not enemies. The need for foreign investment in multiple forms, not just economic or technological investment, has been an enduring feature of Russian history since Ivan III until today. Russia's rulers have long understood Russia's backwardness vis-à-vis its competitors in the West and more recently in the East, even when they rebelled against it and extolled Russia's greatness and *Samobytnost'* (its uniqueness) and had to find a way to maintain that competition without sacrificing what its rulers believed the be the basis of the state, i.e., its autocratic and imperial nature. That is still the case today. According to Trenin, modernization means "Russia using its resources to buy assets in Europe, and Europe supplying Russia with technology." This shows just how deep Europe's wishful thinking is.[212] This is not unlike what Russia's position was in the 1920s and what the New Economic Policy (NEP) was all about in foreign policy.[213] It also shows that the core of Russian foreign policy is not about identity but about the acquisition of tangible resources and material power at home and abroad.

For all these reasons, Rieber duly identified four persistent conditions that are neither immutable nor impersonal but which Russian rulers have invariably confronted through modern history. Their dimensions are subject to change and obviously much depends upon individual rulers, as well as specific conditions of each time and place. But their fundamental attributes persist over time.

These conditions are: relative economic backwardness compared to Western Europe and then America and Japan, a challenge that may now come to include China; permeable frontiers all along the peripheries of state power and thus perennial vulnerability either to physical attack or to cultural-political and ideological trends deemed to be inimical to the security of the state and its ruling order; a multicultural (one could refine this to say multiconfessional and multiethnic) state and society composed of ethno-territorial blocs, frequently located at these vulnerable borderlands; and a persistent sense of cultural marginality relative to its interlocutors.[214] This last point would also include the ongoing Russian sense of being ideologically excluded or subjected to what Moscow likes to call double standards by other powers due to the nature of its political arrangements and policies.[215]

In this context, however, it might be beneficial and of utility to introduce and add a fifth persistent problem that has confronted Russian rulers at least since Ivan the Terrible's times. Indeed, that fifth issue lies at the core of today's foreign policy because of its continuity and because of the universal recognition that it is both state capacity and economic capability that allows a state to play a great role in world affairs. That question is the constant need to adapt and even reform the state structure to the exigencies of international competition. Such competition includes not just war, but both domestic and increasingly global economic, cultural, and technological development. Undoubtedly one of the persistent problems of modern Russian history has been the challenge of building, organizing, and running a state that could cope with the great power challenges of the last 5 centuries whether they are economic, political, cultural, or military.

Although this challenge relates to Rieber's point about a backward economic and social structure, it also stands in its own right if one takes into account the ceaseless activity of Russian rulers since Ivan the Terrible to rebuild the governing state structure to facilitate more effective governance, usable military capability, and economic development. Indeed, Putin's fundamental drive throughout his tenure as president has been the interlinked drive of reviving the economy and restoring the authority and power of the state. For Putin and Medvedev, foreign policy's first priority is to serve the cause of not just keeping Russia out of war and crisis, but of providing the conditions by which its economy and state may be reconstructed.[216] Thus, for Putin, foreign policy has been very much an exercise in stabilizing the external arena so that he can proceed undisturbed with those tasks of economic and governmental revival. In other words, foreign policy has not only been external diplomacy but also a domestic power resource, one increasingly driven by the need to justify and defend a particular political-economic order at home.

This continuing obsession with reorganizing the structure of government can reach almost epic dimensions, as was the case with Lenin, Stalin, and Khrushchev, who constantly reorganized the state, or in Lenin's and Yeltsin's case, first shattered the state they inherited and then rebuilt a new one. But in all these cases, the state building project was decisively shaped by the exigencies of war and/or international relations. That holds true today, for Medvedev's struggle for economic and political modernization is based on his understanding of the rigors of international competition for which Russia is quite poorly organized. The Soviet regime was, after all, a state built to wage class war at home and abroad in an era of total war and often invoked foreign threats or conditions to justify large-scale transformations of the state and of society, e.g., collectivization, the purges, and later on Perestroika. Yeltsin and Putin's efforts to reform state structures, though very different and adapted to different needs are not different in quality. Yeltsin's consuming interest in ensuring his power by gaining Western recognition and acceptance certainly explains much of his foreign policy, which relied upon Western support in both tangible (monetary) and intangible ways in order to silence domestic critics. For him, too, foreign policy was ultimately a domestic power resource. But there is no doubt that one of the major drives of Putin's foreign policy is the demand that the West treat Russia as a great power and show it greater respect than has previously been the case.

Finally, we must understand that when Russian rulers have confronted and will confront these persisting problems in the future, these issues do not come to policymakers' attention as discrete single issues or in the form that Rieber or this author describe them. Political issues never come neatly packaged. Rather, all these problems are bound up with contemporary issues in dynamic and interlinked, often unexpected ways. Indeed, they often may come to policymakers' attention in unpredictable combinations. Thus the quest for an effective state mechanism is and has continually been bound up with the perception that Russia remains behind its competitors or those against whom it constantly measures itself in many, if not all, of the dimensions listed above. Therefore, reform of the state often has been comprehensive in nature in an attempt to address many, if not all, of the sources or manifestations of this backwardness, whether it is in culture or military power. At the same time, many of these reforms have been driven by the exigencies of maintaining an increasingly restive multiethnic and multicultural empire. This drive continues despite the truncation of the empire in 1991 with the Soviet collapse.

The ongoing and at best only partially successful efforts to stabilize the North Caucasus, Russia's most disturbed Muslim frontier, testify to this ongoing continuity. That the linked security threats of terrorism and of Islamism arose in this border area clearly owes much to the failures of the state administration to function well in governing these areas. But if these areas were destabilized, Putin and other high officials have strongly argued that the integrity of the Russian state as a whole would be at risk.[217] Thus the need for comprehensive reconstruction of the state administration in a multiethnic and multiconfessional area vulnerable to ethnic or religious appeals from abroad is very much a priority issue in Russia's overall security policy.

But the continuing failures of the state to function effectively are also tied to the issue of Russia's sense of cultural marginality, for example the "accursed question" of whether Russia is a European, Eurasian, or Asian power or some combination of all or most of these phenomena. Despite the undoubted activity and interest of the Putin regime in enhancing Russia's Asian position and occasional statements to the effect that Russia is a Eurasian state, policymakers still are torn over these issues. Putin, who personally has often cited his own European inclinations, has also given the impression that Asia is something of an afterthought in Russian foreign policy, while his first Foreign Minister, Igor Ivanov, explicitly embraced the idea of Russia as a bridge from Europe to Asia. Analysts such as Alexander Lukin castigate the regime for regarding China and Asia in wholly instrumental terms as a card to be played to get the West's attention and for thus neglecting Asia. Meanwhile, a close examination of the actual policy demonstrates that the executive agents who are to conduct that policy in Asia are continually at odds with each other, thus undermining the entire foundation of Russia's Asian policy.[218] So once again, the debilities of the state as an effective executor of policy reinforce both geopolitical weakness and also the deep-rooted angst over where Russia belongs.

Thus all the five persistent questions are present throughout Russian history until now while the issues tied to them interact continuously and throughout Russian history, highlighting the critical importance of the domestic instrument of the state's effectiveness in Russian foreign policy. An effective state and military is inconceivable without some way of overcoming economic, technological, and cultural backwardness. But, to be sure, the reverse equation also holds, namely that the precondition for overcoming backwardness is an effective state, military, etc. Likewise, the opportunities for expansion due to the presence of divided weak states on the frontier also entail the permeability of Russia's frontiers to both military and ideational threats. From the regime's standpoint this vulnerability to both geopolitical and ideological-cultural penetration is particularly urgent when peoples of another ethnicity, religion, or culture largely inhabit the borders that are at risk.

Neither do these linkages end here. Instead and in fact, they only begin here. The realization of Russia's vulnerability as a multiconfessional and multiethnic empire with restless borderlands vis-à-vis constant but disparate military and political, ideological, or economic threats also relates to the abiding sense of cultural marginality postulated by Rieber. The many complaints about Western double standards apply as much to the unilateral use of force by America as they do to the attacks on Russia's democracy deficit. Those attacks underscore the continuing feeling in Moscow of Russia's cultural marginality as seen from the West, as do the compensatory statements that Russia will never be part of the West whether such statements are uttered in despair or defiance. They are uttered because, as Putin has said in the past, Russia measures itself as a European state and hence by European standards, even if it violates them regularly.

Similarly, the threat of the state's collapse and of its inability to play the role of a great power urgently confronted Putin, by his own admission, when he came to power.[219] Indeed, he has frequently reiterated his belief, beginning in November 1999, in the domino theory that if Chechnya fell, whole provinces would continue to fall, threatening the integrity of the Russian state.[220] These statements clearly unite in a single policy conundrum the threat to the state posed by its ineffectiveness as military and political actor vis-à-vis an insurgency in these restless borderlands. The viability of the Russian state clearly was an issue of the utmost topicality for Putin upon coming to power because he then discerned quite coldly the crisis of the state, which convinced him that Russia was confronting the real threat of dismemberment and disappearance as a great power.[221] Thus he devoted himself from the outset to both the restoration of the state and of Russia as a great power that could ward off the many international challenges that he perceived it faced.[222]

But state reform is not just an effort to stabilize domestic structures against diverse threats occurring in the borderlands. As often as not, it represents an effort to defend Russia's regime against foreign charges of misrule that then repose among disaffected minorities or elites at home. Frequently these defenses must be couched in terms of Western values for this justification to be credible at home and abroad. Indeed, both in the Soviet Union and today under Putin, Russian leaders and spokesmen are constantly at pains to argue that their system represents democracy even though their regime is anything but democratic.

However, such an invocation of foreign values itself testifies to the fact of cultural backwardness and marginality in Rieber's terms. This lagging behind is clearly tied to the problems arising from both Russia's cultural marginality and the unreliability of the peripheries when they come in contract with neighboring states. Thus, historically these perceptions of backwardness, of cultural marginality, or of the borderlands' inquietude have generally not been perceived in isolation from each other. Indeed, they are frequently perceived as a conjoined threat to the stability and integrity of the regime, e.g., Stalin's massive purges among ethnic minorities in the 1930s and 1940s. The quest for an effective governing mechanism is thus naturally bound up with Russia's many efforts to overcome its economic, technological, and cultural backwardness and the restiveness of its minorities in the borderlands. Similarly, the endless obsession with developing a governing structure that can compete with other powers has consistently been bound up with the perception that Russia is in a constant, rigorous, international competition with its interlocutors, imparting the drive of an *a priori* perception of multiple hostile enemies to the overall state building project. This sense that unnamed foreign enemies are always "out there" supporting efforts to weaken, undermine, suppress, and even divide Russia has become a leading trope of elite rhetoric in the last few years.[223]

RUSSIA'S PERSISTING THREAT PERCEPTION

What this means is that despite Russian leaders' efforts to depict their state as a strong, mighty, and united monolith or foreign policy actor, in fact they are constantly haunted by a sense of its weakness and fragility. Once again, observers have long taken note of this duality of stridency and insecurity. Heinrich Vogel alluded to "the typical petrostate combination of presumed omnipotence and yet political insecurity of the leadership."[224] Similarly, Boris Tumanov has written that Russians "simultaneously believe themselves to be the greatest and most oppressed nation on the earth."[225] It is not uncommon for such contradictory emotions to reside in an individual or in a political elite. One way to dispel the fear of marginalization is to insist ever more on Russia's strength and abiding status as a great power (*Velikaya Derzhava*). This linkage of the quest for building a competitive economy and state with foreign threats and this perception of inherent weakness beneath the protestations of great power is most famously expressed in Stalin's 1931 speech that imperial Russia was beaten by everyone for over 100 years because it was backward. But it is no less of a shaping force in Putin's Russia, especially as Putin has increasingly turned to accusing the West of trying to undermine, weaken, exploit, and even break up Russia. Increasingly, Putin's Russia is characterized by the belief that despite the Western perception of a relatively benign threat environment, Russia actually faces mounting and linked threats from within and without. Moreover, at the same time, the West, i.e., primarily America, refuses to take Russia, its interests and objectives seriously and refuses to grant Russia its rightful place as a world power in directing world politics. Even though nobody foresees an attack on Russia or a NATO offensive anytime soon, leading members of the government and armed forces firmly believe that Russia is under siege from both the terroristic threat and from the allegedly conjoined threat of ideological subversion as manifested in the Georgian, Ukrainian, and Kyrgyz revolutions of 2003-05, NATO enlargement, supposed foreign support for Chechen leaders, and now the Arab spring and Western designs upon Libya and Syria.[226]

Therefore they charge that the "enemy is at the gates," that opponents of the Chechen war and proponents of reform constitute "a fifth column," and that unless the elite is totally united behind Putin, the state could disintegrate quite easily.[227] In keeping with the inherited Soviet and KGB mentality and the traditions of projection onto the enemy of your own fears and intentions that was so prominent in Stalin's makeup, they regularly assert that such revolutions are merely the product of external manipulation and subversion, overlooking the domestic roots of such upheavals.

In other words, and confirming Sorokin's fears above, as a fundamental element of its state building process, or more accurately regime formation, the current elite is apparently reviving the Leninist notion of a state challenged from within and without and where the external and internal enemy are essentially one and the same. As happened under Lenin and Stalin, this is basically a call for a perpetual civil war at home or at least a paternalistic state ruling ultimately by force, not to mention a state of siege abroad. Under such circumstances, the almost ritualistic invocation of Russia as a great power and of its revived power in world affairs appears almost as a fetish brandished like a medieval talisman to ward off both real and imaginary apparitions. Consider, for example, the listing of the threats to Russia given by Chief of Staff General Yuri Baluyevsky to a January, 2007 conference of the Academy of Military Sciences on the need for a new defense doctrine. According to Baluyevsky's self-styled comprehensive assessment, the military threats facing Russia are:

> The U.S. military-political leadership's course to preserve its world leadership, and to expand its economic, political, and military presence in regions under Russia's traditional influence; implementation of NATO's expansion plans; introduction into Western practices of military strong-arm actions in circumvention of the generally recognized principles and norms of international law; the existing and potential seats of local wars and armed conflicts, primarily in the direct vicinity of the Russian borders; a possibility of strategic subversion resulting from violations of international arms limitation and reduction agreements or qualitative and quantitative arms build-ups by other countries; proliferation of nuclear and other types of mass destruction weapons, their delivery vehicles and advanced military production technologies in combination with attempts by separate countries, organizations, or terrorist groups to implement their military

and political aspirations; other states' territorial claims to the Russian Federation and its allies; the fight for access to energy resources; international terrorism; unlawful activities by nationalist, separatist, and other organizations directed at destabilizing the internal situation in the Russian Federation; hostile information actions in regard to the Russian Federation and its allies.[228]

These are only the specific military threats, even if their definition is rather broad. Indeed, General M. A. Gareyev (Ret.), the Head of the Academy, echoed Baluyevsky's depiction of the elements of the threats facing Russia, albeit in a somewhat different order. Gareyev stressed that these threats, the breakup of the USSR and of Yugoslavia, color revolutions in the CIS in Georgia, Ukraine, and Kyrgyzstan, etc., show that "principal threats exist objectively, assuming not so much military forms as direct or indirect forms of political, diplomatic, economic, and informational pressure." Moreover, these threats are continuing (obviously from the West) and therefore the state's new military doctrine, and indeed its overall national security policy, of which foreign policy is a critical part, must consider military and nonmilitary threats in their organic unity.[229]

A state whose leaders perceive it to be so comprehensively threatened can hardly account itself a strong or secure state or think of world politics as anything other than a jungle. Hence it is fair to say that Russia under Putin has come to approach world politics on the basis of what the German philosopher Carl Schmitt called the presupposition of enemies and of conflict.[230] Certainly, there can be no doubt that this is the government's threat perception as well, despite undoubted economic success since 2000. For example,

Putin told the G-8 press corps in June 2007 that Russia and the West were returning to the Cold War and added that:

> Of course we will return to those times. And it is clear that if part of the United States' nuclear capability is situated in Europe and that our military experts consider that they represent a potential threat then we will have to take appropriate retaliatory steps. What steps? Of course we must have new targets in Europe. And determining precisely which means will be used to destroy the installations that our experts believe represent a potential threat for the Russian Federation is a matter of technology. Ballistic or cruise missiles or a completely new system. I repeat that it is a matter of technology.[231]

In other words, if the military says it is a threat, it is one. Not only does this reinforce the traditional tendency to see Russia as being comprehensively threatened from abroad, in domestic politics, it gives the General Staff an unchallenged power of threat assessment and formulation. This has decidedly negative tendencies for both domestic politics (budgetary allocations for example) and in foreign policy. Certainly, it reinforces the trend towards marital conceptions of the state and its administrative order, as well as an atavistic and classical Realpolitik approach of zero-sum games to Russian thinking about international relations. In his speeches dating back to 2006 if not 2004 when he accused unnamed foreign elements of seeking "juicy pieces" of Russia, Putin embraced the Baluyevsky-Gareyev threat perception. Putin specifically charged that:

- America is a unipolar hegemon that conducts world affairs or aspires to do so in an undemocratic way (i.e., it does not take Russian interests into account)
- America has unilaterally gone to war in Iraq, disregarding the UN Charter, and demonstrating an "unconstrained hyper use of force" that is plunging the world into an abyss. It has therefore become impossible to find solutions to conflicts (in other words American unilateralism actually makes it harder to end the wars in Iraq and Afghanistan—hardly an incontestable proposition). Because America seeks to decide all issues unilaterally to suit its own interests in disregard of others "no one feels safe," and this policy stimulates an arms race and proliferation of weapons of mass destruction.
- Therefore, we need a new structure of world politics, i.e., multipolarity and nonintervention in the affairs of others. Here Putin cited the Russian example of a peaceful transition to democracy! It should also be noted that Russia hardly has a spotless record with regard to nonintervention as Estonia, Moldova, Ukraine, and Georgia can tell us.
- Putin expressed concern that the Moscow Strategic Offensive Arms Reduction Treaty of 2002 (SORT) may be violated or at least undermined by America, which is holding back several hundred superfluous nuclear weapons for either political or military use. America is also creating new destabilizing high-tech weapons, including space weapons.
- Meanwhile, the Conventional Armed Forces in Europe (CFE) treaty is not being ratified even

though Russian forces are leaving Georgia and only carrying out peacekeeping operations in Moldova. Similarly, U.S. bases are turning up "on our border" (here Putin revealed that for him, the borders of Russia are in fact the old Soviet border since Russia no longer borders either on Romania or Poland).

- America is also extending missile defenses to Central and Eastern Europe even though no threat exists that would justify this. In regard to this program, Putin replied to a question at the 2007 Munich Wehrkunde Conference by saying that:

> The United States is actively developing and already strengthening an anti-missile defense system. Today this system is ineffective but we do not know exactly whether it will one day be effective. But in theory it is being created for that purpose. So hypothetically we recognize that when this moment arrives, the possible threat from our nuclear forces will be completely neutralized. Russia's present capabilities, that is. The balance of powers will be absolutely destroyed and one of the parties will benefit from the feeling of complete security. That means that its hands will be free not only in local but eventually also in global conflicts.[232]

- Moreover, Baluevsky, his successor, General Nikolai Makarov, the General Staff, and Russian officials all regularly argue that, because there is allegedly no threat from Iran, these missile defenses can only be aimed at Russia and at threatening to neutralize its deterrent.[233]
- NATO expansion (the Russian term in opposition to the Western word enlargement) there-

fore bears no relationship to European security but is an attempt to divide Europe and threaten Russia.

- Finally America is seeking to turn the Organization for Security and Cooperation in Europe (OSCE) into an anti-Russian organization and individual governments are also using non-governmental organizations (NGOs) for such purposes despite their so-called formal independence. Thus revolutions in CIS countries are fomented from abroad and elections there often are masquerades whereby the West intervenes in their internal affairs.[234] Recently Prime Minister Putin and his spokesman, Dmitry Peskov, openly claimed that the United States has been planning for 2-3 years in advance to unseat Putin by generating a scandal during the most recent Duma elections in December 2011 and handing out money to oppositionists in support of this goal. While this charge is both totally cynical and delusional, it is entirely consistent with the mentality behind Russian policy.[235] Obviously, this view projects Russia's own politics and policies of interference in these elections (e.g., the $300 million it spent and the efforts of Putin's "spin doctors" in Ukraine in 2004) onto Western governments and wholly dismisses the sovereign internal mainsprings of political action in those countries, another unconscious manifestation of the imperial mentality that grips Russian political thinking and action.

Since then a new consensus has evolved due to Russia's assertive policies, palpable signs of a U.S. decline, the Russo-Georgian war, and the financial crisis that began in 2007 and hit Russia in late 2008. That consensus assumes that Russia has recovered from its travails and is now a recognized, independent great power with the will, capability, and status to be a system-forming power capable of helping to contribute to and help resolve global issues. Second, international politics are on the threshold of a great change, a presumption that includes the perception of U.S. decline. Therefore, the key practical goal is to consolidate Russia as the international defense, financial, political, and security hub in Eurasia, a posture that reflects the intimate linkage between domestic and foreign policy. With this in mind, Moscow seeks to establish Russia as a political hub and model in Eurasia for an alternative path of development other than Western models. Many of Russia's specific policy initiatives, e.g., Medvedev's proposals for a new European security architecture and the unrelenting drive to integrate the CIS around Russia, flow from these assumptions or consensus.[236]

Since 2004, the notion of being surrounded from within and without by the same enemy, i.e., the West, has grown among elites but was based on the previous perception Russia was menaced by terrorists at home who as Putin said were part of a terrorist international from Bosnia to the Philippines. Since 2004, the notion has grown, incited by Putin, that these enemies, increasingly viewed as the West, want to prevent Russia from achieving its rightful place as a great power and dominator of the post-Soviet space and are aiming to subvert the foundations of Russian statehood by misguided and conspiratorial democracy campaigns directed against both the Russian government and its nondemocratic neighbors in the CIS. Indeed, Putin has recently and repeatedly attacked Western forces along with domestic reformers, whom he called jackals for seeking to destabilize Russia, and divide its territory through support for Russian NGOs and the democracy campaign they promote. Putin even likened them to the reformers of the Yeltsin epoch.[237]

Thus the sense of being backward or behind vis-à-vis the West and the corresponding need for a reformed state structure translates into a belief today that foreign policy is not only a way of advancing the national interest, it also is an instrument for ensuring the internal stability of a beleaguered system at home. The articulated concept that Russia's domestic security, i.e., its governmental structure, is at risk from abroad and that the primacy of the domestic threat drives foreign and defense policy not only borrows from Nicholas I's hysteria about liberalism, revolution, and reform and Stalin's notion of capitalist encirclement, it also is a hallmark of the security preoccupations of Third World states whose ramshackle domestic structures are always seen to be at risk of disintegration.[238] Thus in many ways, Russia's national security posture and outlook resembles that of Asian rather than European states, particularly Asian states who are threatened by internal forces and weak legitimacy. Russian experience and overall security policy conforms to the pattern discernible in Asian and Third World states where security is primarily internal security and is recognized as such by all the leaders there. These countries simultaneously confront the exigencies of both domestic state-building, i.e., assuring the regime's internal security and defense against external threats without sufficient means, time, or resources to compete successfully with other more established states. Not surprisingly, their primary concern becomes internal security and their continuation in power, hence the proliferation of multiple military forces, intelligence, and police forces in these countries, often enjoying more resources than do their regular armies, and their governments' recourse to rent-seeking, authoritarian, and clientilistic policies.[239]

These facts possess significant relevance for any discussion of security in the Third World but clearly also for Russia where the security environment perceived by the government is one of "reversed anarchy" as described by Mikhail Alexiev and Bjorn Moeller. Moeller observes that:

> While in modernity the inside of a state was supposed to be orderly, thanks to the workings of the state as a Hobbesian 'Leviathan,' the outside remained anarchic. For many states in the third World, the opposite seems closer to reality — with fairly orderly relations to the outside in the form of diplomatic representations, but total anarchy within.[240]

Similarly, Amitav Acharya observes that:

> Unlike in the West, national security concepts in Asia are strongly influenced by concerns for regime survival. Hence, security policies in Asia are not so much about protection against external military threats, but against internal challenges. Moreover, the overwhelming proportion of conflicts in Asia fall into the intrastate category, meaning they reflect the structural weaknesses of the state, including a fundamental disjunction between its territorial and ethnic boundaries Many of these conflicts have been shown to have a spillover potential; hence the question of outside interference is an ever-present factor behind their escalation and containment. Against this backdrop, the

principle of noninterference becomes vital to the security predicament of states. And a concept of security that challenges the unquestioned primacy of the state and its right to remain free from any form of external interference arouses suspicion and controversy.[241]

Indeed, for these states, and arguably even for transitional states like Russia, internal police forces enjoy greater state resources than do the regular armies, this being a key indicator of the primacy of internal security as a factor in defining the term national security.[242] These points certainly apply to Russia. As Stephen Hanson observes:

> The central puzzle of Russian politics is that fifteen years after the collapse of the USSR, the country still lacks any stable and legitimate form of state order. The result is continuing pervasive political and social uncertainty — concretized in the palpable official fear that independent civil society organizations might promote additional "color revolutions" in Russia or other post-Soviet states and the endless rumors about various unconstitutional or semi-constitutional schemes Putin might employ to stay in power after his formal second term ends in March 2008. Bearing in mind that Russia remains the world's largest country by territory and still possesses thousands of nuclear warheads as well as large stockpiles of chemical and biological weapons of mass destruction, such uncertainty could quickly become a major international problem as well.[243]

These political conditions duly represent some of the reasons why even Russian analysts admit that Russia remains a risk factor in world politics, not the reliable pole of world politics that it claims to be.[244] Thus Vladimir Mau emphasizes that despite the transformation of the past 20 years, the state remains a weak state, one that cannot effectively manage the transition to either a growth economy or democracy.[245] Similarly, Gordon Hahn's study of the Islamic terrorist threat to Russia, primarily in the North Caucasus, flatly states that, "Despite Putin's efforts to recentralize power, Russia remains a weak state, is becoming a failing state, and risks becoming a failed one."[246] Russia's siege mentality, no matter how bizarre it may seem to us, has deep roots in the structure of the state and the real threats to it.

In 2004-05, in the wake of the terrorist attack at Beslan and the Ukraine's Orange Revolution, Russia's frustration with its inability to defend its internal borders or project its system into Ukraine turned into this portrayal of "the enemy at the gates."[247] Vladislav Surkov, Deputy Chief of Putin's presidential administration gave a secret speech explicitly charging that Freedom House is essentially an extension of the Central Intelligence Agency (CIA). Therefore, "it takes an idiot to believe in the humanitarian mission of this establishment." In so describing Freedom House, he used the Russian word *Kontora* or office, the old Soviet term for the KGB.[248] Surkov, like other CIS leaders such as former Ukrainian President Leonid Kuchma, clearly believes that democratic revolutions in CIS states are orchestrated conspiracies against Russia and threats to the stability of the Russian state itself.[249] According to Kremlin commentator Vyacheslav Nikonov, the Kremlin views this revolution as a "refined special operation" or as an externally directed unconstitutional coup against Russia to eliminate its influence in the CIS and replace it with an American presence.[250] Professor Alexei Pushkov of the Moscow State Institute of International Relations called Ukraine a continuation of the "West's strategic line of staging a political takeover of the post-Soviet space."[251] But Surkov was only following his master's and other officials' footsteps in warning that the state is at risk.[252]

This wide-ranging threat perception also embraces Russia's domestic politics as well. Regime spokesmen, e.g., Surkov, also have openly stated that Russia must take national control of all the key sectors of the economy lest they be threatened by hostile foreign economic forces and so called "offshore aristocrats."[253] In other words, this threat perception links both internal and external threats in a seamless whole (as did Leninism) and represents the perception that Western democracy as such is a threat to Russia. Therefore U.S. and Western military power, even if it is not actually a threat, is *a priori* perceived as such.

This outlook affects even those areas where Russia affects to realize a common policy with America, e.g., arms control. For example, Yevgeny Primakov, Yeltsin's Foreign Minister and Prime Minister during 1996-99 and previously head of Russia's Foreign Intelligence Service (SVR), writes in his memoirs that, despite perceptions at the end of the Cold War of an end to enemy relationships with the West, in fact the West has behaved like an enemy, seeking to deprive Russia of its "special role in stabilizing the CIS in order to frustrate hopes for a rapprochement with Russia."[254] Primakov here thus not only postulated the *a priori* existence of foreign enemies, he blamed them for everything that went wrong in Russia and no less implicitly postulates a Russian sphere of influence in the CIS. Those outlooks are clearly by no means his alone. Rather they are shared by most of Russia's contemporary elites and are fundamental to their ideological *Weltanschauung*.

THE MYSTIQUE OF DERZHAVNOST'

Under these circumstances, the centralization and personification of power that have taken place as the critical component of the state-building program must be buttressed by an effort to unify the state and society around the ideology of autocracy and *Derzhavnost'* (Russia's inherent great power status). As Putin has recently observed, this unity is an essential source of Russia's strength.[255] By invoking it, he also has shown his effort to fulfill a key part of the domestic, anti-or counter-reform agenda of that ideology as expressed by Retired General M. A. Gareyev, President of the Russian Academy of Military Sciences.

> A Russia that is mired in division and dissension cannot stand in the modern world. To unify the healthy forces within society and to support a reliable political system one must first define the reasons for the existence of our fatherland. One such uniting factor is the idea of a revival of Russia as a great power, not as a regional one, for Russia stretches across several large regions of Eurasia, and is truly great on a global scale. This greatness is not defined simply by someone's desire, not just by nuclear weapons, or the country's size. It is determined by historical traditions and the real-world needs for the development of Russian society and state. Either Russia will be a strong, independent. and unified state, uniting all peoples, republics, territories, and areas in the territory of Eurasia, which is in the interests of all mankind, or she will scatter into pieces, becoming a source of many conflicts. Then the entire international community will be unable to cope with a situation in which Eurasia is brimming with weapons of mass destruction. Either Russia will be a great power, or she will not exist at all. There is no other alternative.[256]

Similarly, Dutch Scholar John Loewenhardt reported in 2000 that despite the fact that Russia's alleged status as a leading pole in global affairs was then understood to be increasingly more rhetorical than real:

> In one of our interviews a former member of the Presidential Administration said that the perception of Russia as a great power 'is a basic element of the self-perception of high bureaucrats.' If a political leader were to behave as if Russia was no longer a great power, there would be 'a deeply rooted emotional reaction in the population.'[257]

This concept that Russia is simultaneously both inherently a great power and a state that deserves to be seen at home and abroad as such or as an empire in order to survive — even if this can only be asserted irrationally and not by empirical demonstration — is embodied in the term *Derzhavnost'* (tellingly, a word that emerged into popularity only in the 1990s when the concept it denotes was under fierce attack). As conservatives endlessly insist, going back to the famous line of the 19th century poet Fedor Titutchev "*Umom Rossiiu ne poniat'*" ("Russia cannot be understood by the mind"), this belief in Russia's great power destiny is an article of faith not subject to critical thinking.[258] This irrationalist and organicist approach to the nation not only aims to dissuade criticism by invoking a mantra of near theological belief, it also is a long-standing refuge for conservatives and reactionaries against the rationalism embedded in classical and modern Liberalism. By trying to banish any hope of understanding Russian politics through critical rational analysis, it also typically overcompensates for the fear that if Russia is not a great power and not seen as such, then it will be nothing. Putin, Yeltsin, and many other figures like former Foreign Minister and Prime Minister Evgeny Primakov have repeatedly echoed this sentiment about Russia as an inherent great power that must act independently of other "poles" of the international system.[259] For example, upon becoming Foreign Minister in 1996 Primakov told Rossiyskaya Gazeta that:

> Russia's foreign policy cannot be the foreign policy of a second-rate state. We must pursue the foreign policy of a great state . . . the world is moving toward a multipolar system. . . . In these conditions, we must pursue a diversified course oriented toward the development of relations with everyone, and at the same time, in my view, we should not align ourselves with any individual pole. Precisely because Russia itself will be one of the poles, the 'leader-led' configuration is not acceptable to us.[260]

As Primakov's words suggest, not only is this concept of Russia as a great power inextricably tied to the idea of Russia as an independent unconstrained actor in world politics, just as the Tsar is not constrained by anything at home, the *Derzhavnost'* concept entails Russia as a leader in world politics forming its own solar system of states around it.[261] Equally importantly, this concept is tied to a particular notion of Russia's identity as an actor in world politics where either it is acknowledged as a great power or, its leaders fear, it counts for nothing. But this attitude's practical implications as seen in ongoing demands for bases throughout the CIS, obstruction in the CIS frozen conflicts, and the energy crises with Ukraine and Belarus are unmistakably imperial in consequence. The *Derzhavnost'* concept betokens a belief that Russia is an empire sufficient unto itself and thus above all of the other rules of international life, precisely what it attacks Washington for doing.[262] As Trenin observed, Moscow wants to create its own solar system of international relations, replete with client states, independent of the West.[263]

Thus *Derzhavnost'* postulates Russia as an empire freed of external constraints that form a chain of states around it because while it is a great power, they are not and therefore cannot defend their sovereignty. Certainly, Russian scholars know full well that Russia's elites have long continued to see the Russian state in imperial terms. As Alexei Malashenko observed in 2000, Russia's war in Chechnya is logical only if Russia continues to regard itself as an empire.[264] More recently, Russian political scientist Egor Kholmogorov has observed that:

> 'Empire' is the main category of any strategic political analysis in the Russian language. Whenever we start to ponder a full-scale, long-term construction of the Russian state, we begin to think of empire and in terms of empire. Russians are inherently imperialists.[265]

If Russia is such an empire, then it becomes clear why EU or NATO membership becomes a threat to Russian sovereignty. For as Deputy Foreign Minister Ivan Ivanov stated in 1999:

> Our country is not in need of affiliation with the EU. This would entail loss of its unique Euro-Asian specifics, the role of the center of attraction of the re-integration of the CIS, independence in foreign economic and defense policies, and complete restructuring (once more) of all Russian statehood based on the requirements of the European Union. Finally great powers (and it is too soon to abandon calling ourselves such) do not dissolve in international unions — they create them around themselves.[266]

It is noteworthy that in Ivanov's list of reasons for not joining the EU empire preceded independence suggesting the deeply rooted belief among Russian elites that if Russia is not an empire, it is not a state. Hence, it is not surprising that Ivanov outlined here the goal, alluded to by Trenin above, of creating a solar system around Russia. But the quest for great power and empire is the fetish invoked by Russian statesman throughout the ages to ward off the nightmare of being marginalized and no longer being a great power. This nightmare haunts the imagination of Russia's political elite and undoubtedly is one of the most primordial psychological and cognitive drivers of Russian foreign policy, even if it postulates only two possible outcomes for Russia, great or even super-power status, or oblivion and marginalization.[267] Indeed, in pursuing this mirage of being a great power that can act unconstrainedly in world affairs, Putin has sought to copy the Bush administration's doctrine of preemption or preventive war to justify its unlimited right to military intervention in the CIS with rather less justification than did President George Bush, for there have been no foreign-based attacks upon Russia.[268]

So this concept of *Derzhavnost'* is inextricably linked to the current notion of Russia being a sovereign democracy, with the emphasis on Russia's sovereignty and independence, the supposed primary goal of its foreign policy.[269] Of course, it is this sovereignty, independence, and hence great power status that are most at risk from the aforementioned threats. In other words, Russia increasingly defines its independence and sovereignty as being an inherently anti-Western and neo-imperial project.

This concept of *Derzhavnost'* did not only recently spread throughout the elite. Instead, it is in the nature of the historical legacy handed down from ruler to ruler despite the historical rupture generated by the Bolshevik Revolution of 1917. Nicholas II's Prime Minister, Count Sergei Witte, famously said that he did not recognize Russia but rather the Russian empire. After him, Stalin in 1937 underlined the profound sense of historical continuity in the minds of Russian policymakers through the ages concerning the vital necessity of retaining the Russian empire and the accompanying status of a great power. At Defense Minister Voroshilov's villa, in November 1937, Stalin remarked that:

> The Russian Tsars did much that was bad. They robbed and enslaved the people. They led wars and seized territory in the interests of the landowners. But they did one good thing — they put together an enormous Great Power. . . . We inherited this Great Power. We Bolsheviks were the first to put together and strengthen this Great Power, not in the interests of the landowners and capitalists, but for the toilers and for all the Great People who make up this Great Power.[270]

The congruence of Stalin's remarks with contemporary thinking and his backhanded glorification of Tsardom's imperial legacy is no accident. Thus Alexei Malashenko of the Carnegie Endowment observes that in relation to the war in Chechnya, Russia's war in Chechnya is logical only if Russia continues to regard itself as an empire.[271] Kholmogorov's observation only brings that observation into the present.[272]

Similarly, the contemporary publicist close to the regime, Stanislav Belkovsky, writes that, "In 2004-08, the foundations of the Russian nation must be laid.

Our nation has only one destiny—imperial."[273] Yeltsin's former prime minister, Egor Gaidar, forthrightly charged that an organized movement of imperial nostalgia that seeks to reject the need to come to terms with the loss of empire is rampant among today's officialdom and society. Gaidar states that this attitude invokes arguments that are all too reminiscent of German conservatives in the Weimar Republic, and represent one of the greatest challenges to Russia's security and stability.[274]

This adherence to *Derzhavnost'* was also a foundation point for Tsarist statesmen, who possessed what Dietrich Geyer calls "the power elite's traditional sense of imperial prestige."[275] Geyer was writing about the historical period of the 1860s, an era of reform, threatened loss of autocratic power, instability, and renewed imperialism and state nationalism. This era in particular has been the historical reference point for much of contemporary Russian policy because it was another period of weakness abroad and domestic reform that ended in an increasingly aggressive nationalism comparable to the contemporary scene.[276] Indeed, contemporary evidence suggested then that much of Russia's foreign policy standing in the decade after the Crimean War stemmed from its efforts at reform, and that reform was also driven by the need to maintain its standing in Europe.[277] This underscores the enduring linkage between domestic and foreign policy in Russian history. Consequently, we can see that many of the key reference points and foundations of Putin's foreign and domestic policies are rooted in a deeply rooted elite and quite possibly in the popular consciousness of the historical continuity of the Russian state and of its interests. Likewise, there is a similarity between the cycles of reform and counter-reform that were enacted then and are being reenacted now and using similar arguments against reform points to underlying continuities in Russian history.[278]

Russian foreign policy under both Yeltsin and Putin is inextricably tied to the assertion of this great power project that depends on the unification of the population around a counter or anti-reform program. It is no accident, to use a Stalinist neologism, that Russia's anti-Westernism takes its point of departure from the same time, as does the end of democratizing and liberalizing reforms. Indeed, as we shall see, the enemies of reform consciously appealed to *Derzhavnost'* to derail liberalizing reforms. Under both rulers, foreign policy has become very much a resource for domestic politics to ensure their regime's hold on power.

At the same time, this formulation of Russia as an inherent and intrinsic great power is tied to an organic view of the state as a unified supra-ethnic political entity. Proponents of this view, like Gareyev, clearly believe that *Derzhavnost'*, i.e., great power ranking and status is *the only alternative* for Russia. Thus, they connect liberalization, not to mention democracy, and their inherent tendency to deconcentrate state power with the essential end of Russia as an independent state. They regard all challenges to this ideal of *Derzhavnost'* as a challenge if not threat to Russia's ability to conduct an independent foreign policy and survival as a state or great power (the two are essentially the same identity).[279] Likewise, they regard all efforts at democracy as being akin to treason or at least as representing a threat to Russia's great power destiny and standing, not to mention their own power.

The *Derzhavnost'* or imperial concept of Russia's destiny and status has always been a rock, if not the rock, upon which major reform has foundered in Russia going back at least to the Decembrist revolt of 1825, if not earlier. It also is tied to a belief that Russia is a unique actor whose path must be defined by its statist, authoritarian, centralized, and anti-liberal, not to mention anti-democratic, tradition. In effect, like the outlook of German conservatives before World War II, this view of Russia as an inherent great power for reasons that are often invoked and not analyzed is connected to a view of Russia as having a unique *Sonderweg* (other way). Like German conservatism, and quite ironically in view of its unrestrained championing of Russia's uniqueness, this view is almost wholly derived from the tenets and categories of German Romantic and conservative thinking in the early 19th century as well as Russian Slavophilism. At the same time, the continuing emphasis on an imperial stance also derives from Russia's own historical experience as an empire as interpreted through those earlier German and then Slavophile categories of thought.

Contemporary Russian leaders have clearly inherited this worldview. Indeed, to judge from Putin's domestic and foreign policies, they can only conceive of the state as an imperial, even pre-modern formation based on an organic unity around the Tsar that rejects political dissent, and which is unified by a common ideology and a state religion.[280] Certainly the way Putin's succession by Medvedev as president has worked out indicates that the state remains essentially pre-modern in its structure, if not its leaders' mentality. The authoritarian coalition's deeply held vision of Russia's having to be a great power or nothing denotes the constant sense of inner insecurity and even illegitimacy of the elite and of the state it has created. This inner sense of insecurity and even of illegitimacy are particularly striking when Russia compares itself or is compared to European processes and standards, hence both the sense of cultural marginality and the often outsized and outlandish claims made to compensate for that sense of marginality. Indeed, the frequent resort to Soviet-like rhetoric and threats against parties who conduct policies deemed to be inimical to Russian interests betrays, as much as anything, both weakness and an awareness of weakness and even an awareness that Russia does not compare favorably with its peers. Therefore, one function of these heavy-handed threats and rhetoric is overcompensation: a way of telling its elite and population that Russia still is a great power and trying to impress this fact upon Russia's interlocutors. Meanwhile, at the same time this great power status must be an imperial, even opulent one in both style and substance. In order to awe any potential rivals at home or abroad and reassure the elite of the awesome power of the Tsar or now of Putin. It must be imperial to awe potential enemies as well as subjects with Russian power, to provide security against all manner of internal and external threats, and to confirm the self-image and unconstrained power of the elite and the Tsar or President.

Consequently and despite the fact that Putin has explicitly said he is against the restoration of any official ideology, his regime has manufactured one based on a concept of Russia's being an inherent great power and relying on the forces of Putin's autocracy and cult of personality, the exaltation of the Russian Orthodox Church as the state church, and on a growing intolerance to foreigners expressed as an official state nationalism. Arguably, the similarity of this ideology to Nicholas I's official nationality that exalted autocracy, orthodoxy, and nationality, and to Stalin's cult of personality is not accidental.[281] Neither are the now visible similarities to the Brezhnev era, as suggested above.[282] Indeed, the continuing need for some state ideology that defends Russia against its supposed ideological as well as political enemies and justifies its system to both domestic and foreign audiences has been a feature of Russian statecraft since Ivan the Terrible sought to create such an ideology in the 16th century. Certainly Peter the Great, Catherine the Great, and then Nicholas I each explicitly sought to forge a body of ideas that justified their policies to both sets of audiences. The effort to form an ideology during Yeltsin's presidency and Putin's subordinates' propagation of an ideology called "sovereign democracy" continues that tradition.

Unfortunately, along with the penchant for ideological justification of its regime, the Putin government has taken over much of this perception of being under siege from domestic as well as foreign enemies, and not just terrorists. In this regard, Putin has inherited the outlook that characterized those elements of the Soviet system that could not reconcile themselves fully to the post-Soviet world and, like Putin, regard the collapse of the Soviet Union as the greatest geopolitical disaster of the 20th century. Just as Lenin instituted a "state of siege," first within Russian Social Democracy and then in world politics, Putin's Russia now seems to postulate that same condition, albeit in a less intense form of polarization. Nonetheless, the similarities between the Putin regime as of late 2007 and its Soviet predecessors are clear to Russian writers.

PUTIN'S FOREIGN POLICIES AS DOMESTIC POWER RESOURCE

Analysts of Putin's foreign policies must understand that, first and foremost, it was and is an instrument for stabilizing the regime's ability to pursue a domestic agenda of reconstructing centralized power, even autocracy. Foreign policy's task has been to prevent situations that could obstruct the rebuilding of autocracy (i.e., the state's authority conceived of in a hierarchical power vertical) while elevating Russia's effective status and power in world affairs. Then that strengthened state could pursue a more aggressive and independent foreign policy, thereby continuing the reciprocal relationship between domestic and foreign policy. Numerous statements by Putin underscore that he has understood foreign policy until now in just such a light, i.e., as having the primary task of allowing him to pursue his domestic agenda for reconstructing Russia as a great and centralized power that in turn would then allow him to pursue a stronger foreign policy.

Neither is there any doubt that Putin was the most popular and successful politician in Russia, even if much of that popularity is manufactured or the product of fear of repression. In 2007, a poll gave him an almost 80 percent popularity rating![283] Indeed, he may be the most successful and legitimately popular ruler in Russia since Stalin. As Dale Herspring has written about Putin, "He is in charge. Indeed, one could argue that Putin is more in charge than any post-Stalin leader of the Soviet Union."[284] This fact makes his regime's manipulations so that an open election not take place all the more discouraging. Still, like his Soviet and Tsarist predecessors, Putin rules, as many analysts have noted, as a Tsar, i.e., he is not responsible to anyone nor is his state subordinated to any control by law or any other institution.[285] In this regard as in so many others, Putin's Russia represents a reinvigoration if not reincarnation of what we have called above the Muscovite paradigm.

Putin has marginalized every other possible source of political initiative in Russian society and substituted state control over all of these potentially influential segments of Russian society so that there can be no effective challenges to either domestic or foreign policy. Indeed, as early as 2005 his entourage boasted that they had smashed all institutions and bureaucratic "veto groups" as well as any hope of autonomous political action from the Duma. Igor Bunin, Director General of the Center for Political Technologies, stated then that Putin's reforms have aimed at converting the entire state system into a mono-centric administration where he and his entourage have all the power. In such a system, conflicts within the bureaucracy are supposedly absent because it is vertically integrated. Hence the government becomes a technical instrument rather than a policy initiator, a task reserved for Putin and his entourage in the presidential chancellery.[286] Foreign observers note that he has essentially deinstitutionalized the state, robbing all other organs but the presidential administration of any real vitality.[287]

In fact, as the traditional Muscovite paradigm and Russian history clearly suggest, the effort to completely depoliticize Russia and its policies only means that fierce political conflict has moved into the bosom of the bureaucracy from where it cannot easily be dislodged. The succession struggle of 2007-08 with visible as well as invisible political struggles between the rival bureaucratic clans who make up the leadership, going all the way to arrests and political murders, underscores the opacity of Russian politics. These struggles are inherent in the Russian political system, and we find numerous instances of them among the Tsars and in the Soviet period. For example, Stalin deliberately fostered such conflicts, as did his predecessors and successors, to retain their full prerogative of power. As bureaucratic conflicts have not abated but have migrated to interclan rivalries among the power structures of the regime and Putin's entourage (the so called Silolvye Struktury and the Siloviki) a fierce domestic rivalry among these clans or factions invariably occurs, as has always been the case in modern Russian politics. But the regular state does not perform better nor is the public directly involved as anything other than an object of manipulation.

So, paradoxically, the strengthening of the power vertical results in the strengthening of the Kremlin and of centralized power, but it is not clear that the regular organizations of the state, including the Ministry of Foreign Affairs, perform any better or that the state really is more effective.[288] If anything, it may be less effective as a direct result of Putin's policies of centralization of power at the top. Consequently, this program ultimately remains insufficient to fully revive the economy or improve the state mechanism as much as Putin wants. In this respect, Putin's Russia follows in the tradition of Russian political history where all modern efforts to revive the Muscovite paradigm have led to the same outcome. In many, if not all of these cases, efforts to reform the system, either towards greater centralization or towards greater liberalization within the framework of the system, often achieved sub-optimal results. Improvements did not reach full fruition, and that frustration carried within it the seeds of further crisis. In other words, Putin's success suggests that the system he has consolidated will relatively soon reach a dead end, even if it continues along its own entropy or inertia.

As part of this agenda of strengthening the central power structures, Putin and his underlings have also attempted to disseminate through Russian society not just a cult of Putin's personality (thereby confirming Marx that when history repeats itself the first time – in this case, under Stalin – it occurs as tragedy; while in the second case – as is now the case under Putin – it returns as farce) but also an ideology that emphasizes Putin's autocracy, the legitimacy of this autocracy in terms of support for the regime by the Orthodox Church, and third, an aggressive doctrine of state nationalism. They also evidently believe that have achieved or at least profess their desire for a result that has eluded Russian rulers since Nicholas I, namely officialdom's recurrent dream of a perfectly integrated vertical hierarchy that functioned strictly as a machine acting on orders from the top and implementing them in quasi-military style and hierarchy. Because this machine supposedly incarnated the Tsar's position as superseding all factional, partial, and sectoral interests, and subordinating everyone to the service of the state, it was equally supposedly wholly depoliticized and had only the state's true national interest at heart. Only the state truly represents the genuine national interest as opposed to partial and sectoral elite interests, which invariably entail oligarchy and ultimately the loss of empire and great power status. Of course, this system left those atop the machine with all the power and opportunities to conceal their self-serving rent-seeking under the cloak of supposedly being the embodiment of the national interest. Russian and foreign analysts therefore rightly underscore the persistence of Tsarist mores and structures in contemporary Russian political life.[289]

Whereas it is debatable how successful Putin has been in creating an effective state in domestic politics, Putin is fortunate that his foreign policy — in great contrast to that of his predecessor, Yeltsin — has hitherto been a key factor in his success, especially as discordant voices have either been silenced or marginalized. Foreign observers like Hryhoriy Nemyria, when he was Director of the Kyiv-based Center for European and International Studies, have stated that, "A significant part of Putin's legitimacy lies in his ability to control developments in Russia's near abroad."[290] Indeed, in foreign policy, perhaps more than in any other aspect of his rule, Putin is more totally in charge since foreign policy historically and in present day Russia is regarded as a "Tsarskoe Delo," something worthy of the Tsar's or ruler's attention (and, of course, a conscious evocation of the continuity in official mores from Russian history). In other words, all the freelancers of the preceding decade have been suppressed, in Khodorkovskii's case, forcibly, and no doubt exemplarily. This does not only mean that Putin decides policy arbitrarily, although he certainly could if he wanted to. But it does suggest that his prerogative is the ultimate and most authoritative, if not irreversible, one.

In this respect, Putin's power, as numerous commentators have noted, resembles that of a Russian Tsar, if not the power of the General Secretary of the Communist Party of the Soviet Union.[291] For example, in September 2001 after the terrorist attacks on the United States, Putin convened a meeting of his 20 other senior advisors on the issue of whether or not to help Washington in Central Asia and to what degree. Of these advisors, 18 opposed the idea of supporting the U.S. military presence in Central Asia and Afghanistan, two abstained, and Putin supported the idea of offering such help with no strings attached. Not surprisingly, his decision prevailed. This authoritative role of the ruler typifies Russian history (one need only remember that Tsar Alexander II forced through the emancipation of the serfs even when the State Council opposed key provisions of the plan[292]) and certainly held true under Yeltsin, who as Bobo Lo and Dmitri Trenin observe, in truly autocratic fashion "regarded foreign policy as essentially the sum total of his personal relations with foreign leaders."[293]

Thus, foreign policy success and even the appearance of success means Russia's self-perception as a great power being accepted abroad and that Russia can also behave with a free or at least strong hand in world affairs are critical factors in sustaining Putin's domestic power and authority.[294] In turn, domestic needs that go beyond the drive for economic recovery, to include the stabilization of a particular form of rule and accompanying political economy, drive foreign policy. This drive is most noticeable in the CIS — the former Soviet republics and what was called in the 1990s the near abroad.[295] Here, Russia assiduously promotes the perpetuation or extension of its own form of rule to those states, not least because the perpetuation of domestic Tsarism requires its perpetuation and extension to the next tier of states as well. But this also means that because so much of it is driven by domestic factors, or to influence them, much of Russian foreign policy emerges out of an unregulated struggle between or among rival bureaucracies and can only be decided by Putin.

A key part of both Putin's domestic and foreign policies has consequently been his unrelenting efforts to present himself in a particularly appealing image to his audience. Apart from Putin's personal motives (and such cults only betray the inner insecurity of the leader and his need for adulation as well as his subordinates' belief that he needs it and that by stimulating it, he will reward them), this image campaign naturally correlates with the efforts to forge a cult of personality and ideology that justifies his policies to domestic and foreign audiences, all part of a very long-standing Russian political tradition. Like the trained KGB agent that he was, Putin has consistently striven to present himself to different audiences as he thinks they wish to see him, an ability that Stalin also possessed in abundance. Thanks to his success in this endeavor, abetted by a managed and suppressed Russian media, Putin has enjoyed great domestic and foreign success in coming across to others as a decisive, practical, reliable, and predictable steward of Russian national interests. One need only cite his strong personal ties with President George Bush, German Prime Minister Gerhard Schroeder, and Italian President Silvio Berlusconi as examples. But there are other examples as well. Still, perhaps more importantly, at home his success has been even greater. By portraying himself to the public as a sober, tough-minded, masculine, and plain speaking, no-nonsense leader who was devoted to Russia's recovery and prosperity as a great power and by suppressing alternative voices, Putin tapped into one of the deepest emotions among Russian political figures, namely the obsession that as Yeltsin said, "Russia deserves to be a great power." (It is crucial here to note the distinction between the present tense and the conditional in this statement). He also tapped into the deep-seated belief that Russia needs a Tsar "who can make the Boyars jump," i.e., a man who can be frightful in the exercise of power.

An example of the ongoing relevance of Rieber's approach may be found in an examination of Putin's "state-building" activities in the light of the linkages between domestic and foreign policy highlighted by this historical approach. By accepting this threat assessment, which was already strikingly outlined in the Defense and National Security Doctrines of 2000 and the Foreign Policy Concept in earlier forms, Putin has formally ratified the unity of concept between his perception of the need to reform the state and the sense of being under threat domestically and externally from more advanced powers.[296] Putin's quest for an effective governing mechanism, seen in the light of Russian history, evokes memories of previous Tsarist and Soviet attempts to create a similarly ideal type of state against the threat of revolution from abroad that could exploit Russia's backwardness. This constant search for an effective and responsive "power vertical" continues to this day under Putin. It is not just that what followed in the wake of Communism was a much more chaotic state that encountered great difficulty in formulating both its identity as a state and an effective foreign policy, although this certainly was the case. Rather, we also see as well a similar obsession in the case of Nicholas I and his elite, as well as his successors, in perfecting the mechanism of government.[297] The many upheavals generated by Peter the Great and Stalin had as their aims, among other things, strengthening Russia's capacity to ward off perceived foreign threats.

As Nicholas I's obsession was with revolution and with the threat that an ineffective state structure both stimulated desires for radical change and could not monitor those who might act upon such desires, so clearly is Putin's obsession with suppressing dissent, unifying the state, and imparting to it a quasi-military and police outlook of unquestioning discipline and service to the state a response to the threat that he and his associates perceive in democracy and in Western superiority. A man and regime that claims that the collapse of the Soviet Union was the greatest geopolitical disaster of the 20th century cannot see democratization as a source of strength for his Russia. Neither will his foreign policy recommend democracy's extension to the newly independent states of the former Soviet Union.

Therefore, these similarities between Putin's "militocracy" and Nicholas' cult of quasi-military order are surely more than personal idiosyncrasies.[298] Nicholas' rule was in itself a continuation of trends observable under Paul I, his father, and his brother, Alexander I. Those contemporary challenges to Russia that find their reflection or response in ongoing reorganization of the state are not just the preparation of a state for war against what is now perceived as a growing military threat and the maintenance of a vigorous and effective diplomacy in service to the regnant national interest of the day. Rather, they are part of a tradition of visualizing the state as an idealized military-type organism that should be pervaded by the same spirit of self-discipline and selfless service that is to be expected in the army. This is because the fundamental paradigm of Russian state power, as we shall see below, is one that is inherently pre-modern, patrimonial, martial, and demonstrably suboptimal as regards great power competition over time.[299]

This tradition generally privileged military power and standing over broad-based economic and technological development.[300] The latter's purpose was invariably to provide for the former. Nevertheless, as Rieber rightly observes, awareness of backwardness has haunted Russian rulers for centuries and stimulated all their efforts to catch up, not just in economic and technological terms, but also, as noted above, in remodeling the government to compete with Russia's interlocutors. The reforms of Peter the Great, Catherine the Great, Alexander I, Alexander II, the Witte and Stolypin reforms, Lenin's War, Communism, and Stalin's revolutions all had the critical goal of preparing the Russian state for war and international rivalry, and were openly admitted as having such objectives. Gorbachev's Perestroika and foreign policies aimed to reduce the defense burden upon the state and reorient it for more successful economic competition in world politics.

Consequently, Putin's and his team's realization of the primacy of the need to develop a modern economy in Russia and use economic power as the foundation of Russia's global standing marks a significant innovation in Russia's history. Only after economic stability was achieved did we see the meaningful increases in defense spending that are now taking place. But the ultimate goal of advancing the great power standing and capacity of the state is entirely traditional in nature as is the belief that the state must lead this process by itself without reference to indigenous self-standing social networks.[301] It is too soon to tell if this priority of economics represents a long-term and stable trend but one that could or will give way, as may increasingly be possible, to renewed emphasis on overt military great power rivalry. Certainly the statist and dirigiste notion of economic development that now prevails in Moscow augurs badly for democracy or for optimal economic growth but strongly for the perpetuation of the Muscovite paradigm with its emphasis on defense. That trend is highly likely to lead logically to an increase in defense rivalry and political tensions with other major powers, as has historically been the case. The substantial rise in defense spending and increasingly military cast of the rivalry with America is a warning sign in this regard. For if the end result of Putinism is a renewed militarization, then the innovative aspects of his legacy will diminish while the assertion of traditional practices and policies will have triumphed.

TOWARDS A PUTIN SYNTHESIS

We have mentioned "Putin's" foreign policy and not by accident. Putin inherited a state in disarray. He himself certainly believed it was in danger of disintegration from terrorist threats and from the ambitions of regional politicians and oligarchs.[302] One of the clear signs of disarray was the fact that foreign policy under Yeltsin reflected the inability of the state to centralize control over Russian politics as a whole. Yeltsin was never fully able to establish his control of that policy, for all his efforts to that end. As a result, foreign policy was very often made by diverse forces, often acting on their own to impose their own agenda or create "facts on the ground."

Military and right wing political and public opinion frustrated openings to Japan in 1992.[303] This had major consequences for it left China, a very different state with a very different and certainly not pro-democratic government as Russia's main partner in East

Asia.[304] Russian energy policies during the 1990s were also clearly a matter of competition among private and state companies and governmental bureaucracies, making it difficult for Moscow to devise a coherent and viable energy program to meet both the opportunities and rising foreign challenges it began to encounter during the 1990s.[305] Finally in 1999, General Anatoly Kvashnin, Chief of the General Staff, initiated the Russian Army's march on Pristina and blindsided both the Ministry of Defense and the Ministry of Foreign affairs, even though this march almost landed Russia in a conflict with NATO. Slightly earlier, Yeltsin's first Foreign Minister, Andrei Kozyrev, though loyal and idealistic, failed to gain control over foreign policy or impress observers with his competence.[306] Kozyrev's ministry, for example, publicly stated in 1992 before Yeltsin aborted his trip to Japan that it had given Yeltsin 14 options for his negotiations over the Kurile Islands before his proposed visit to Japan, a sure sign of incompetence.[307] Not surprisingly, his and Yeltsin's pro-American policies were under constant attack from forces opposed to Yeltsin's economic and political reforms and from the armed forces. Indeed, the Foreign Ministry itself remained largely unreformed despite Kozyrev's appointment.

These factors, coming on top of the catastrophic economic conditions and political strife of the 1990s not only led to a revival of conservatism, based on the axis of Russian state patriotism, they ensured that the pro-Western foreign policy associated with Yeltsin and Kozyrev were under constant pressure from a growing conservative and statist-oriented coalition.[308] By 1992-93, as official documents like the 1993 foreign policy concept indicate, that pro-Western policy was in steady retreat.[309] But the precedent of politicizing foreign policy success or failure in the domestic debate as a way to enhance or reduce the government's standing was firmly established. Putin has learned from this experience and his curtailment of the media and establishment of a consensus from above by virtue of establishing unchallenged power based on a notion of Russian state greatness has enabled him to stifle debate on his foreign policies. Thus today there is no public consensus as to what Russian national interests either are or should be because there is no debate on these issues. Rather, there is an incessant beating of the drums for state nationalism or patriotism manipulated from Putin's and now Medvedev's office in order to squelch unfettered public debate.

Meanwhile, the chaos surrounding foreign policy during the 1990s allowed other actors to exploit the policy vacuum for their own interests. Unilateral military operations in the Caucasus and Moldova, ostensibly in the name of peacekeeping or peacemaking, exploited ethnic divisions in Georgia and Moldova and Azeri-Armenian tensions over Nagorno-Karabakh to create lasting proto-states in these areas, often garrisoned or protected by Russian military forces. These officers and politicians associated with them and these proto-states not only asserted their political and psychological interest in seeing Russia act as a great power and imperial policeman in the former Soviet Union, they also benefited and still benefit handsomely from the many opportunities for corruption provided by these proto-states. Consequently, they have created a situation of permanent tension in the Caucasus, particularly with Georgia but also with the West that arguably does not benefit Russian interests as a whole. For instance, it remains an open question if Georgia would be so anti-Russian and pro-Western if Russia had helped broker a viable solution to the conflicts in Abkhazia and South Ossetia. In that case, there would be much less East-West rivalry here and also a much more stable situation-confronting Russia throughout both the North Caucasus and Trans Caucasus.

This chaos abated somewhat during the late 1990s as a stronger hand in foreign policy by Yevgeny Primakov gradually restored some order to policymaking and veered towards the elite consensus on attempting to build a multipolar world where Russia engaged everyone and acted or portrayed itself as acting as a great independent power on a global stage. Although ultimately this approach, too, failed for lack of resources with which to play this role, it more nearly reflected the emerging elite consensus and helped to make the foreign policy debate in Russia less partisan. But it did so at the price of making it also less democratic. Foreign policy was now firmly established as a state activity carried out by the President and his team and removed from partisan political debate and influence.

Putin has built upon this achievement as well as the long-standing tradition in Russian history (that Yeltsin tried but only partially succeeded in realizing) that foreign policy is the Tsar or dictator's prerogative alone. His success is due both to his ability to silence domestic debate, largely through repression and manipulation of public opinion through the media, and to his successes. But even if one argues that his policies have frequently not succeeded in achieving their foreign policy goals, they have done so in a domestic context, i.e., in consolidating an elite consensus and an elite form of rule, not necessarily in achieving greater stature or security for Russia. Arguably, today Russia may be wealthier and in some ways more powerful, but it also is more distrusted than it should be or needs to be. Thus this apparent success has been purchased at the price of a reversion to a traditional form of Russian rule, i.e., autocracy, which has repeatedly been shown to be inherently sub-optimal in ensuring Russia's lasting security and stability. For all the innovative qualities of Putin's foreign policies and notwithstanding the newness of today's international environment, not enough of Igor Ivanov's argument is being validated, while too much of Sorokin's lament appears to have come true and still remains the case in both domestic and foreign policy.

ENDNOTES - CHAPTER 2

1. Igor S. Ivanov, *The New Russian Diplomacy*, Washington, DC: The Nixon Center and Brookings Institution, 2002, pp. 21-22.

2. Sorokin is quoted in Michael Kimmelman, "Putin's Last Realm to Conquer: Russian Culture," *New York Times*, December 1, 2007, p. A9.

3. The most recent example is Putin's Article, "Russia Muscles Up-the Challenges We Must Rise to Face," January 16, 2012, available from *premier.gov.ru*.

4. Neil Robinson, "Patrimonial Capitalism and the International Financial Crisis," *Journal of Communist Studies and Transition Politics*, Vol. XXVII, No. 3-4, September-December, 2011, pp. 434-455; Brian D. Taylor, *State Building in Putin's Russia: Policing and Coercion After Communism*, Cambridge, MA: Cambridge University Press, 2011; Richard Hellie, "The Structure of Russian Imperial History," *History and Theory*, Vol. XLIV, No. 4, December, 2005, pp. 88-112; Peter Baker and Susan Glasser, *Kremlin Rising: Vladimir Putin's Russia and the End of Revolution*, New York: Scribner's, 2005, p. 417; Steven Rosefielde, *Russia in the 21st Century: the Prodigal Superpower*, Cambridge, MA: Cambridge University Press, 2004; Marshall T. Poe, *The Russian Moment in World History*, Princeton, NJ: Princeton University Press, 2003; Stefan Hedlund, *Russian Path Dependence*, London, UK; Routledge, 2005;

Emil Pain, "Will Russia Transform Into a Nationalist Empire?" *Russia in Global Affairs*, Vol. III, No. 2, April-June, 2005, pp. 71-80; Stephen Kotkin, "It's Gogol Again," Paper Presented as part of the project, *The Energy Dimension in Russian Global Strategy*, James A. Baker III Institute for Public Policy, Rice University, Houston, TX. These are only a few of the authors who now see the vitality of the Tsarist metaphor as a means of explaining Putin's Russia; Center for Strategic and International Studies, Washington, DC: Praeger, 2004; Richard Pipes, *Russia Under the Old Regime*, New York: Scribner's 1975; Stephen Blank, *Rosoboroneksport; Its Place in Russian Defense and Arms Sales Policy* Carlisle, PA: Strategic Studies Institute, U.S. Army War College, 2007; Harley Balzer, "Confronting the Global Economy After Communism: Russia and China Compared," Paper Presented to the Annual Convention of the International Studies Association, Honolulu, HI, March 1-5, 2005.

5. Alexei Arbatov, "Russia's Own Imperial Road," Natasha Bubnova, ed., *20 Years Without the Berlin Wall: A Breakthrough to Freedom*, Moscow, Russia: Carnegie Center, Carnegie Endowment for International Peace, 2011, p. 32.

6. Evgenia Chaykovskaya, "Peskov: Comparing Putin to Brezhnev Is a Good Thing," *Moscow News*, October 5, 2011, available from *themoscownews.com/politics/20111005/189096032.html*.

7. Heinrich Vogel, "The Putin System," *Internationale Politik Transatlantic Edition*, No. 1, 2002, p. 4; Fred Weir, "Putin's Duel With the Bureaucrats," *Christian Science Monitor*, February 22, 2002, confirms this; and "Russia's General Staff Resisting Putin's Force Reforms," *Jane's Defence Weekly*, February 14, 2002, p. 10, confirms this for the military.

8. Vitaly V. Shlykov, "Does Russia Need a General Staff," *European Security*, Vol. X, No. 4, Winter, 2001, pp. 45-83; Stephen Blank, "From Kosovo to Kursk: Russian Defense Policy From Yeltsin to Putin," *Korean Journal of Defense Analysis*, Vol. XII, No. 2, Winter 2000, pp. 231-273; Dale R. Herspring, *The Kremlin and the High Command: Presidential Impact on the Russian Military from Gorbachev to Putin*, Foreword by David M. Glantz, Lawrence, KS: University of Kansas Press, 2006.

9. Moscow, *Nezavisimaya Gazeta*, in Russian, November 29, 2000, Foreign Broadcast Information Service (*FBIS*) *Soviet* (*SOV*), November 29, 2000.

10. David M. MacDonald, "A Lever Without a Fulcrum: Domestic Factors and Russian Foreign Policy, 1905-1914, " Hug Ragsdale, ed., *Imperial Russian Foreign Policy*, Washington, DC, and Cambridge, UK: Woodrow Wilson Center Press and Cambridge University Press, 1993, p. 281.

11. Ivan Safranchuk, "Russian Views on Missile Defense," *Pugwash Occasional Paper*, Vol. II, No. 2, March, 2001, pp. 38-42.

12. *Ibid.*

13. Arbatov, p. 54.

14. Andrei Ryabov, "No Institutions," Bubnova, ed., *20 Years Without the Berlin Wall*, p. 79.

15. Nikolay Petrov, "Stalin's System Reduplicated," Moscow, Russia: *Carnegie Moscow Center* April 21, 2004, available from *www.carnegie.ru/en/pubs/media/70274*.

16. Gregory Carleton,"History Done Right: War and the Dynamics of Triumphalism in Contemporary Russian Culture," *Slavic Review*, Vol. LXX, No. 3, Fall 2011, p. 617.

17. Taylor.

18. Dmitri Trenin, "Overview of the History of Russian Foreign Policy (1992-2010), Bubnova, ed., *20 Years Without the Berlin Wall*, pp. 245-246.

19. Jonathan Steinberg, *Bismarck: a Life*, New York: Oxford University Press, 2011.

20. Trenin, "Overview," pp. 245-248.

21. *Ibid.*

22. Celeste A. Wallander, "The Challenge of Russia for U.S. Policy," Testimony before the Committee on Foreign Relations, United States Senate, June 21, 2005.

23. Alexander Golts and Tonya Putnam, "State Militarism and Its Legacies,: Why Military Reform Has Failed in Russia," *International Security*, Vol. XXIX, No. 2, Fall 2004, pp. 121-159; Aleksandr' Golts, *Armiya Rossii: 11 Poteryannykh Let*, Moscow, Russia: Zakharov, 2004.

24. "Russian Finance Minister Alexei Kudrin Resigns," BBC News Europe, September 26, 2011, available from *www.bbc.co.uk/news/world-europe-15064866*.

25. Andrei Illarionov, "The Siloviki in Charge," *Journal of Democracy*, Vol. XX, No. 2, April, 2009, p. 72.

26. Stephen Blank, "Rumors of War: Russia and Its Neighborhood," Forthcoming in *World Defence Systems*, 2012.

27. Taylor.

28. Sergei V. Lavrov, "Containing Russia: Back to the Future," July 25, 2007, available from *www.mid.ru/brp_4.nsf/e78a48070f12 8a7b43256999005bcbb3/8f8005f0c5ca3710c325731d0022e227?Open Document*.

29. Ministry of Energy of the Russian Federation, *Energeticheskaya Strategiya Rossii Na Period do 2020 Goda*, Moscow, Russia, 2003.

30. *Ibid.*

31. Roman Kupchinsky, "Energy and Russia's National Security Strategy," *The Progressive Realist*, May 19, 2009, available from *www.progressiverealist.org/blogpost/energy-and-russias-national-security-strategy*.

32. Ministry of Energy of the Russian Federation, *Energeticheskaya Strategiya Rossii Na Period do 2030 Goda*, Moscow, 2009.

33. "Russia Gains a New Uzbek Client," *Jane's Foreign Report*, December 8, 2005; "Uzbek Airfield Is Made Available to Russia in Emergencies," *Ferghana.ru Information Agency*, December 22, 2006.

34. Stephen Blank, "The Naval Dimension of the New Great Game," *World Defence Systems*, Vol. IX, No. 2, 2007, pp. 34-40.

35. Blank, "The Naval Dimension of the New Great Game," pp. 34-40.

36. Zoltan Barany, *Democratic Breakdown and the Decline of the Russian Military*, Princeton, NJ: Princeton University Press, 2007; Herspring, *The Kremlin and the High Command*, Foreword by Glantz.

37. Sergei F. Platonov, *Time of Troubles: A Historical Study of the Internal Crisis & Social Struggles in Sixteenth & Seventeenth-Century Muscovy*, John T. Alexander, trans., Lawrence, KS; University Press of Kansas, 1970.

38. *Report of the Defense Science Board Task Force on Nuclear Capabilities: Report Summary*, Washington, DC: Office of the Under Secretary of Defense for Acquisition, Technology, and Logistic, December, 2006, pp. 11-12; Conversations with officers from U.S. European Command (USEUCOM), Cambridge, MA, November 26, 2007.

39. Alfred Rieber, "How Persistent Are Persistent Factors?" *Ibid.*, pp. 205-277; Alfred J. Rieber, "Persistent Factors in Russian Foreign Policy: An Interpretation," Hugh Ragsdale, ed., *Imperial Russian Foreign Policy*, Washington, DC, and Cambridge, MA: Woodrow Wilson Center Press and Cambridge University Press, 1993, pp. 315-359.

40. David R. Cameron and Mitchell A. Orenstein, *Post-Soviet Authoritarianism: The Impact of International Actors, Linkages, and Alliances*, Paper Presented to the Annual Convention of the American Political Science Association, Seattle, WA, September 3, 2011.

41. *Ibid.*, p. 16.

42. Samuel Charap and Alexandros Petersen, "Reimagining U.S. Interests and Priorities in Post-Soviet Eurasia," Paul J. Saunders, ed., *Enduring Rivalry: American and Russian Perspectives on the Former Soviet Space*, Washington, DC: Center for the National Interests, 2011, pp. 5-7.

43. Nazrin Mehdiyeva, "New Man in the Kremlin: What Future for Russian Foreign Policy?" *The International Spectator*, Vol. XLIII, No. 2, June, 2008, p. 25.

44. Oksana V. Goncharova, *Russia and Europe: Opportunities and Practical Realizations,* Paper Presented to the Standing Group on International Relations Conference, Stockholm, Sweden, 2010, p. 10.

45. "Interview with Vyacheslav Nikonov, President of the Politika Foundation," Moscow, Russia, *Rossiyskaya Gazeta*, in Russian, July 26, 2007, *Open Source Center, FBIS SOV*, July 26, 2007.

46. Putin, "Russia Muscles Up — The Challenges We Must Rise to Face"; Fleming Splidsboel-Hansen, "Past and Future Meet: Aleksandr' Gorchakov and Russian Foreign Policy," *Soviet Studies*, Vol. LIV, No. 3, 2002, pp. 377-396.

47. Andrey Kolesnikov, "United Stolypin Front — How Vladimir Vladimirovich Gave Petr Arkadyevich's Speeches," Moscow, *Kommersant Online*, in Russian, July 14, 2011, *Open Source Center, FBIS SOV*, July 15, 2011; Alexei Makarin, "The Kremlin: the Sovereign and the Premier," Moscow, Russia, *Yezhednevnyi Zhurnal*, in Russian, July 28, 2011, *FBIS SOV*, July 29, 2011.

48. Andrei P. Tsygankov, *Russia's Foreign Policy: Change and Continuity in National Identity,* Lanham, MD: Rowman & Littlefield Publishers, 2006.

49. "Russia Says U.S. Deserves No Explanation on Syria Arms, Rejects Sanctions," *Al-Arabiya News*, January 19, 2012, available from *english.alarabiya.net/articles/2012/01/18/189034.html*.

50. Timofei Bordachev, "Toward a Strategic Alliance," *Russia in Global Affairs*, No. 2, April-June, 2006, p. 3.

51. Stanislav Secrieru, *Russia's Quest for Strategic Identity*, Rome, Italy: NATO Defense College, 2006, p. 19.

52. Arkady Moshes, "EU-Russia Relations: Unfortunate Continuity," Foundation Robert Schuman, *European Issues*, No. 129, February 24, 2009, pp. 2-3.

53. Moscow, *Interfax*, in English, August 17, 2011, *FBIS SOV*, August 17, 2011.

54. Semyon Novoprudsky, "Soviet Warehouse," Moscow, Russia, *www.Gazeta.ru*, in Russian, August 17, 2011, *FBIS SOV*, August 17, 2011.

55. Dmitri Furman, "A Silent Cold War," *Russia in Global Affairs*, IV, No. 2 (April-June, 2006), 73.

56. *Ibid.*

57. Celeste A. Wallander, "Russian Transimperialism and Its Implications," *The Washington Quarterly*, Vol. XXX, No. 2, 2007, pp. 117-118.

58. Robert Larsson, *Nord Stream, Sweden and Baltic Sea Security*, Stockholm, Sweden: Swedish Defense Research Agency, 2007; Robert Larsson; *Russia´s Energy Policy: Security Dimensions and Russia´s Reliability as an Energy Supplier*, Stockholm, Sweden: Swedish Defense Research Agency, 2006; Janusz Bugajski, *Cold Peace: Russia's New Imperialism*, Washington, DC: Center for Strategic and International Studies, Praeger, 2004; Richard Krickus, *Iron Troikas*, Carlisle, PA: Strategic Studies Institute, U.S. Army War College, 2006; Keith C. Smith, *Russian Energy Politics in the Baltics, Poland, and the Ukraine: A New Stealth Imperialism?* Washington, DC: Center for Strategic and International Studies, 2004.

59. Sergei Medvedev, "Power, Space, and Russian Foreign Policy," Ted Hopf, ed., *Understandings of Russian Foreign Policy*, University Park, PA: Penn State University Press, 1999, pp. 46-49.

60. Michael Emerson, "Do We Detect Some Neo-Finlandization in the Eastern Neighborhood?" *CEPS Commentary*, May 28, 2009, available from *www.ceps.be*.

61. *Ibid.*

62. *Ibid.*

63. Thomas Graham, *Resurgent Russia and Purposes: A Century Foundation Report*, New York: The Century Foundation, 2009, pp. 23-25.

64. "Bulgaria, Russia Clear Out Diplomatic Scandal," September 1, 2009, available from *www.novinvite.com*.

65. Judy Dempsey, "KGB-Trained Hungarian Has NATO Role," *New York Times*, February 4, 2008.

66. Edward Lucas, *The New Cold War: Putin's Russia and the Threat to the West*, London, UK: Palgrave Macmillan, 2008; Larsson, *Nord Stream, Sweden and Baltic Sea Security*; Larsson; *Russia's Energy Policy*; Marshall Goldman, "Putin, Petroleum, Power, and Patronage," Washington, DC: Jamestown Foundation, 2006, available from *www.jamestown.org/media/events/single/?tx_ttnews%5Btt_news%5D =133&tx_ttnews%5BbackPid%5D=19&cHash=6*; Smith; Author's conversations with members of European foreign ministries and intelligence services, 2008; Anita Orban, *Power, Energy, and the New Russian Imperialism*, Washington, DC: Praeger, 2008; Edward Lucas, *The New Cold War: Putin's Russia and the Threat to the West*, London, UK: Palgrave Macmillan, 2008; Larsson, *Nord Stream, Sweden and Baltic Sea Security*; Larsson, *Russia's Energy Policy*; Bugajski, *Cold Peace*; Krickus, *Iron Troikas*; Valery Ratchev, "Bulgaria and the Future of European Security," paper presented to the SSI-ROA Conference, "Eurasian Security in the Era of NATO Enlargement," Prague, the Czech Republic, August 4-5, 1997; Laszlo Valki, "Hungary and the Future of European Security," *Ibid.*; Stefan Pavlov, "Bulgaria in a Vise," *Bulletin of the Atomic Scientists*, January-February 1998, pp. 28-31; Moscow, Russia, *Izvestiya*, in Russian, June 19, 1997, in *FBIS SOV*, pp. 97-169, June 18, 1997; Sofia, Bulgaria, *Novinar*, in Bulgarian, April 10, 1998, in *Foreign Broadcast Information Service, Eastern Europe (FBIS EEU)*, April 13, 998, pp. 98-100.

67. Gundar J. King and David E. McNabb, "Crossroads Dynamics in Foreign Policy: The Case of Latvia," *Problems of Post-Communism*, Vol. LVI, No. 3, May-June, 2009, p. 39.

68. Temur Basilia, "Eurasian Commentary," in Jan H. Kalicki and Eugene K. Lawson, eds., *Russian-Eurasian Renaissance? U.S. Trade and Investment in Russia and Eurasia,* Stanford, CA: Stanford University Press, 2003, p. 166.

69. "Putin Speaks Out Against "Exporting Capitalist Democracy," *ITAR-TASS News Agency,* April 11, 2003, retrieved from Lexis-Nexis; for an example from Turkmenistan, see Gennady Sysoev, "Saparmyrat Niyazov Seeks Protection," Moscow, Russia, *Kommersant,* in Russian, April 11, 2003, *FBIS SOV,* April 11, 2003.

70. Basilia, p. 163.

71. Sabine Fischer, "Ukraine As a Regional Actor," Sabine Fischer, ed., *Ukraine: Quo Vadis,* Chaillot Pape No. 108, Paris, France: Institute for Security Studies, European Union, 2008, p. 119.

72. Lilia Shevtsova, "Russia's Choice: Change or Degradation?" *Paper Presented to the Conference on Russia,* Carlisle, PA, September 26, 2011, p. 4.

73. Dmitri Furman, "A Silent Cold War," *Russia in Global Affairs,* Vol. IV, No. 2, April-June, 2006, p. 72.

74. Dmitry Furman, "A Cold War Without Words: Democratic Camouflage Keeps Russia from Properly Formulating Its Real Policy in the CIS," Moscow, Russia, *Nezavisimaya Gazeta,* in Russian, March 27, 2006, *FBIS SOV,* March 27, 2006.

75. Rieber, "Persistent Factors in Russian Foreign Policy: An Interpretation," pp. 315-359; Rieber, "How Persistent Are Persistent Factors?" pp. 205-277.

76. Robert Amsterdam, "Russia's Velvet Privatization," available from *www.robertamsterdam.com,* contains a reprint of Shvartsman's interview with Kommersant, December 20, 2007.

77. Clifford Gaddy and Barry W. Ickes, "Resource Rents and the Russian Economy," *Eurasian Geography and Economics,* Vol. XLVI, No. 8, 2005.

78. Hellie, "The Structure of Russian Imperial History," pp. 88-112; Baker and Glasser, *Kremlin Rising*, p. 417; Rosefielde, *Russia in the 21st Century*; Poe, *The Russian Moment in World History*; Hedlund, *Russian Path Dependence*; Pain, "Will Russia Transform Into a Nationalist Empire?" pp. 71-80; Kotkin, "It's Gogol Again"; Pipes, *Russia Under the Old Regime*; Blank, *Rosoboroneksport*; Balzer, "Confronting the Global Economy After Communism: Russia and China Compared."

79. Clifford G. Gaddy and Barry W. Ickes, "Russia after the Global Financial Crisis," *Eurasian Geography and Economics*, Vol. LI, No. 3, 2009, pp. 281-311; Clifford G. Gaddy, "The Russian Economy in the Year 2006, *Post-Soviet Affairs*, Vol. XXIII, No. 1, 2007, p. 2.

80. James Sherr, "The Russia-EU Energy Relationship: Getting it Right," *The International Spectator*, Vol. XLII, No. 2, 2010, p. 56.

81. Michael Shurkin, *Subnational Government in Afghanistan*, Santa Monica, CA: Rand Corporation, 2011, p. 5, available from *www.rand.org*.

82. Shoichi Ito, Vladimir I. Ivanov, Zha Daojiong, "China, Japan, and Russia: The Energy Security Nexus," Niklas Swanstrom, ed., *Conflict Prevention and Conflict Management in Northeast Asia*, Uppsala Silk Road Studies Program, Uppsala, Sweden: Uppsala University, 2005, pp. 139-140, available at *www.silkroadstudies.org*.

83. Stephen Blank, "Russia's Geoeconomic Future; The Security Implications of Russia's Political and Economic Structure," *Journal of Slavic Studies*, Vol. XXIV, No. 3, 2011, pp. 351-395.

84. Author's Conversations with Foreign diplomats and officials in 2007-08; Wikileaks from U.S. embassy.

85. Clifford G. Gaddy and Barry W. Ickes, "Russia after the Global Financial Crisis," *Eurasian Geography and Economics*, Vol. LI, No. 3, 2009, pp. 281-311.

86. Testimony of Andrei Illarionov before the House Committee on Foreign Affairs, at the hearing "From Competition to Collaboration: Strengthening the U.S.-Russia Relationship," February 25, 2009, available from *www.house.gov*.

87. "Poland Sees Expansion in Russian Spying Network," *RIA Novosti*, June 26, 2007.

88. *FORUM/Moscow/Russia Internet*, in Russian, May 24, 2008, *FBIS SOV*, May 24, 2008.

89. "Ukraine, Russia Expel Diplomats," July 30, 2009, available from *www.upi.com*.

90. *FBIS SOV*, December 13, 2004.

91. Viktors Baublys, "Bank May Lose Lieutvos Rytas," Vilnius, *Vilnaius Diena*, in Lithuanian, August 8, 2009, *FBIS SOV*, August 8, 2009.

92. *FBIS SOV*, October 1, 2007.

93. Jurga Tvaskiene, "Russia does Not Need 'Exposed' Friends," Vilnius, *Lieutvos Zinios*, in Lithuanian, September 11, 2009, *FBIS SOV*, September 11, 2009.

94. *Ibid*.

95. Moscow, *ITAR-TASS*, in English, September 9, 2009, *FBIS SOV*, September 9, 2009.

96. Richard J. Krickus, "The Presidential Crisis in Lithuania: Its Roots and the Russian Factor," *Occasional Papers of the East European Studies Institute*, No. 73, Washington, DC: Wilson Center, 2004; Vilnius, *BNS Internet Version* in English, September 21, 2007, *FBIS SOV*, September 21, 2007; Kaunas, *Kauno Diena Internet Version*, in Lithuanian, September 20, 2007, *FBIS SOV*, September 21, 2007.

97. Tallinn, *Eesti Express internet Version*, in Estonian, October 1, 2007, *FBIS SOV*, October 1, 2007.

98. Budapest, *Magyar Hirlap Online*, in Hungarian, August 6, 2009, *FBIS SOV*, August 6, 2009.

99. Budapest, *Hungary Around the clock*, in English, August 24, 2009, *FBIS SOV*, August 24, 2009; Budapest, *Magyar Hirlap Internet*

Version, in Hungarian, December 14, 2007, *FBIS SOV*; "Hungary, Austria: A Continuing Energy Rivalry in the Balkans," August 6, 2008, available from *www.stratfor.com*.

100. Ference Kepecs, "Hungarian Maneuvering in the Draw of three Power Centers," Budapest, *Nepszava*, in Hungarian, July 31, 2008, *FBIS SOV*, July 31, 2008; Budapest, *MTI*, December 10, 2007, *FBIS SOV*, December 10, 2007.

101. Budapest, *MTI*, in English, November 14, 2008, *FBIS SOV*, November 14, 2008; Budapest, MTI, in English, September 25, 2008, *FBIS* SOV, September 25, 2008.

102. Vladimir Prybylovsky, Natalya Morar, Ilya Barabanov, and Yevgeniya Albats, "From Petersburg to Reykjavik: Whose Money Is Rescuing Iceland," *Compromat.ru Internet*, in Russian, October 20, 2008, *FBIS SOV*, October 20, 2008; Dan Bilefsky, "Despite Crisis, Wealthy Russians Are Buying Up Coastal Montenegro," New *York Times*, November 1, 2008, available from *www. nytimes.com*.

103. Jan Gazdik, "In Czech Republic Russians Are Reactivating Agents From the Cold War Period," Prague, *IDnes.cz Online*, in Czech, August 25, 2009, *FBIS SOV*, August 25, 2009.

104. Gazdik, *FBIS SOV*, August 25, 2009.

105 . *Ibid.*; Erik Tabery and Ondrej Kundra, "The Big Spying Game: What Was Behind the Expulsion of Two Russians from the Czech Republic"? Prague, *Respekt.cz Online*, in Czech August 24-2009-August 30-2009, *FBIS SOV*, August 31, 2009; Lenka Ziamalova, "Interview With Lucas Dobrovsky," Prague, *Hospodarske Noviny Online*, in Czech, August 21, 2009, *FBIS SOV*, August 25, 2009; Prague, *Czech Happenings*, in English, August 21, 2009, *FBIS SOV*, August 25, 2009; Prague, *Czech Happenings*, in English August 27, 2009, *FBIS SOV*, August 27, 2009; Prague, *CTK*, in English, August 31, 2009, *FBIS SOV*; "Russia, Czech Republic: Trading Diplomatic Expulsions," August 18, 2009, available from *Stratfor.com*.

106. Gregory Feller, and Brian Whitmore, "Czech Power Games: How Russia is Rebuilding Influence in the Former Soviet Bloc," *Radio Free Europe Radio Liberty*, September 25, 2010.

107. *Ibid.*

108. Prague, *CTK,* in English, August 31, 2009, *FBIS SOV*, August 31, 2009.

109. Tabery and Kundra, *FBIS SOV*, August 31, 2009.

110. Lenka Ziamalova, "Interview With Lucas Dobrovsky," *FBIS SOV* August 25, 2009.

111. Lenka Ziamalova, "Interview With Deputy Foreign Minister Thomas Pojar," Prague, *Hospodarske Noviny Online*, in Czech, September 25-28, 2009, *FBIS SOV*, September 28, 2009.

112. Jana Klimov and Janek Kroupa, "Nuclear Waste Storage Facility at Temelin Being 'Built' By Russian Consul," Prague, *IDnes.cz, in Czech,* September 17, 2009, FBIS *SOV*, September 17, 2009.

113. Feller and Whitmore.

114. Jeremy Druker, "Prague: The 'Second Infiltration'," International Security Network, September 14, 2009, available from *www.isn.ethz.ch.*

115. *Ibid.*

116. Caversham, *BBC Monitoring*, in English, August 13, 2009, *FBIS SOV*.

117. Smith; Author's conversations with members of European foreign ministries and intelligence services, 2008; Anita Orban, *Power, Energy, and the New Russian Imperialism*, Washington, DC: Praeger, 2008; Edward Lucas, *The New Cold War: Putin's Russia and the Threat to the West*, London, UK: Palgrave Macmillan, 2008; Larsson, *Nord Stream, Sweden and Baltic Sea Security*; Larsson; *Russia's Energy Policy*; Bugajski *Cold Peace*; Krickus, *Iron Troikas*; Valery Ratchev, "Bulgaria and the Future of European Security,"

paper presented to the SSI-ROA Conference, "Eurasian Security in the Era of NATO Enlargement," Prague, August 4-5, 1997; Laszlo Valki, "Hungary and the Future of European Security"; Stefan Pavlov, "Bulgaria in a Vise," *Bulletin of the Atomic Scientists*, January-February 1998, pp. 28-31; Moscow, *Izvestiya*, in Russian, June 19, 1997, in *FBIS SOV*, pp. 97-169; Sofia, *Novinar*, in Bulgarian, April 10, 1998, in *FBIS EEU*, pp. 98-100, April 13, 1998.

118. Ugroza Kremlya,"April 7, 2008, *Radio Free Europe Radio Liberty Newsline*, April 8, 2008, available from *www.kommersant. com*; "Putin Hints At Splitting Up Ukraine, " *Moscow Times*, April 8, 2008; "Putin Threatens Unity of Ukraine, Georgia," *Unian*, April 7, 2008, available from *www.unian.net*.

119. "Ugroza Kremlya."

120. Stephen Blank, "The Values Gap Between Moscow and the West: the Sovereignty Issue," *Acque et Terre*, No. 6, 2007, pp. 9-14 (Italian), pp. 90-95 (English), cites many examples of such statements and policies.

121. Available from *www.kremlin.ru/eng/text/speeches/2009/ 08/11/0832_type207221_220745.shtml*.

122. *Ibid*.

123. Dmitri Trenin, *Post-Imperium: a Eurasian Story*, Washington, DC: Carnegie Endowment for International Peace, 2011, p. 29.

124. Moscow, *Vesti TV*, in Russian, February 6, 2007, *FBIS SOV*, February 6, 2007.

125. Blank, "The Values Gap Between Moscow and the West."

126. Trenin, *Post-Imperium*, pp. 13-14.

127. Blank, "The Values Gap Between Moscow and the West," pp. 90-95.

128. "Army Chief Warns Poles: If You Want U.S. Shield, Buy Gas Masks," *Russian Courier*, July 16, 2007, available from *www. russiancourier.com/en/news/2007/07/16/75153/*.

129. Stephen Blank, "A Scandal in Serbia," *Eurasian Daily Monitor*, Forthcoming.

130. Koba Bendeliani, "Interview With Sergei Markov," *Kviris Palitra*, June 26, 2006, cited in *Johnson's Russia List*, June 26, 2006, available from *www.cdi.org/russia/johnson/*.

131. Moscow, *Vesti TV*, in Russian, February 6, 2007, *FBIS SOV*.

132. Charles Clover, "Ukraine Looks East," *FT.com*, January 21, 2001, available from *www.ft.com*; Charles Clover, "Kiev Warned on Neutral Policy," *Financial Times*, July 12, 2001, p. 2.

133. *Radio Free Europe Radio Liberty Newsline*, from Radio Mayak, Moscow, October 11, 2005, available from *www.ft.com*.

134. "Russian Minister's Military Pact Comment Seen as Warning to Rice in Central Asia," NTV, Mir, October 11, 2005, retrieved from Lexis-Nexis.

135. "Moscow, NTV in Russian, July 2, 2005, *FBIS SOV*.

136. Clover, "Ukraine Looks East," p. 2; Clover, "Kiev Warned on Neutral Policy," p. 1.

137. Riga, *Baltic News Service*, December 20, 2006.

138. For Russian policy towards Bulgaria, see Ratchev, "Bulgaria and the Future of European Security"; Laszlo Valki, "Hungary and the Future of European Security"; Stefan Pavlov, "Bulgaria in a Vise," *Bulletin of the Atomic Scientists*, January-February 1998, pp. 28-31; Moscow, *Izvestiya*, in Russian, June 19, 1997, in *FBIS SOV*, pp. 97-169, June 18, 1997; Sofia, *Novinar*, in Bulgarian, April 10, 1998, in *FBIS EEU*, pp. 98-100, April 13, 1998.

139. "Russian Ambassador Plays Down Impact of Ukrainian NATO Membership," *Interfax News Agency*, Moscow, June 8, 2002.

140. "Russian Ambassador: We Will Not Allow US Presence in Caspian, "*Baku Today*, June 12, 2003; Stephen Blank, "Central Asia's Great Base Race," *Asia Times Online*, December 19, 2003.

141. *Ibid.*

142. Viktor Janszo, "Hungary's Eyes on Russia Again," Budapest, *Magyar Hirlap*, in Hungarian, March 30, 2007, *FBIS SOV*, March 30, 2007; Attila Pinter, "Interview With Zsolt Nemeth," *Ibid*; Peter Dunail, "Confrontational Policy Leads Nowhere," Budapest, *Nepszabasdag*, in Hungarian, January 5, 2007, *FBIS SOV*, January 5, 2007; Andreas Desi, "This Is a New Russia," *Ibid.* March 30, 2007, *FBIS SOV* March 30, 2007.

143. Vladimir Socor, "Putin Offers Ukraine "Protection" for Extending Russian Black Sea Fleet's Presence," *Eurasia Daily Monitor*, October 30, 2006.

144. *Ibid.*

145. *Ibid.*

146. *The Jamestown Monitor*, June 18, 2000.

147. Steven D. Roper, "Federalization and Constitution-Making as an Instrument of Conflict Resolution," *Demokratizatsiia*, Vol. XII, No. 4, Fall 2004, p. 536.

148. Alexei K. Pushkov, "Missed Connections, "The *National Interest*, No. 89, May-June, 2007, pp. 52-55.

149. Moscow, *Interfax*, in English, October 19, 2011, *FBIS SOV*, November 19, 2011.

150. "Senior MP Advises Turkmenistan to Stick with Russia to Avoid Libya's Fate," Moscow, Russia, *Interfax*, November 15, 2011; also available from *BBC Monitoring*.

151. Vladimir Socor, "Moscow Issues Trans-Caspian Project Warning," *Asia Times Online*, December 2, 2011, available from *www.atimes.com*.

152. Maura Reynolds, "Moscow Has Chechnya Back—Now What?" *Los Angeles Times*, June 19, 2000.

153. Quoted in Boris Rumer, "Central Asia: At the End of the Transition," Boris Rumer ed., *Central Asia At the End of Transition*, Armonk, NY: M. E. Sharpe & Co. Inc., 2005, p. 47.

154. *Strategiia Razvittia Otnoshenii Rossiiskoi Federatsii s Evropeiskim Soiuzom na Srednesrochnuiu Perspektivu (2000-2010) Diplomaticheskii Vestnik*, November 1999, available from *www.ln.mis.ru/ website/dip_vest.nsf*, items 1.1., 1.6, and 1.8.2000, cited in Hannes Adomeit and Heidi Reisinger, *Russia's Role in Post-Soviet Territory: Decline of Military Power and Political Influence*, Oslo, Norway, Norwegian Institute for Defence Studies, Forsvarstudier No. 4, 2002, p. 5.

155 . Taylor; Hellie, "The Structure of Russian Imperial History," pp. 88-112; Baker and Glasser, *Kremlin Rising*, p. 417; Rosefielde, *Russia in the 21st Century*; Poe, *The Russian Moment in World History*; Hedlund, *Russian Path Dependence*; Pain, "Will Russia Transform Into a Nationalist Empire," pp. 71-80; Kotkin, "It's Gogol Again"; Pipes, *Russia Under the Old Regime*; Blank, *Rosoboroneksport*; Balzer, "Confronting the Global Economy After Communism: Russia and China Compared."

156. Paul J. Saunders, "Managing U.S.-Russian Differences in the Former Soviet Space," Paul J. Saunders, ed., *Enduring Rivalry: American and Russian Perspectives on the Former Soviet Space*, Washington, DC: Center for the National Interests, 2011, p. 74.

157. Sergei Ivanov, "Russia Must Be Strong," *Wall Street Journal, January 11, 2006, p. 14*.

158. Yuliya Alekhina, "America preparing for World Internet War," Moscow, Russia, *Komsomolskaya Pravda*, in Russian, July 28, 2011, *FBIS SOV*, July 29, 2011; Jim Sciutto, "The Police State Playbook: An Introduction," *World Affairs journal*, July-August, 2011, available from *www.worldaffairsjournal.org/articles/2011*; Andrei Soldatov, "Kremlin's Plan to Prevent a Facebook Revolution," *The Moscow Times*, in English, February 28, 2011, FBIS *SOV*.

159. Col. A. A. Strel'tsov (Ret.), "Basic Goals of Government Policy in Information Wars and Battles," *Military Thought* (English), XX, No. 2, 2011, p. 36.

160. "Dmitry Medvedev Held a Meeting of the National Anti-Terrorism Committee in Vladikavkaz," February 22, 2011, available from *eng.kremlin.ru/transcripts/1804*.

161. Tatiana Stoyanova, "Are 'They' the Main Threat to Russia?" Moscow, Russia, *politkom.ru*, in Russian, February 25, 2011, *FBIS SOV*.

162. I. V. Stalin, "The Policy of the Soviet Government on the National Question in Russia," *Pravda*, October 10, 1920; Joseph Stalin, *Marxism and the National Question: Selected Writings and Speeches*, New York: International Publishers, 1942, p. 77.

163. Roman Szporluk, ed., *The Influence of East Europe and the Soviet West on the USSR*, New York: Praeger Publishers, 1975; Vladimir D. Shkolnikov, "Modernization and Russian Democracy," *Fletcher Forum of World Affairs*, Vol. XXIX, No. 2, Summer, 2005, pp. 21-25.

164. *Ibid.*

165. Stephen Blank, "We Can Live Without You: Dialogue and Rivalry in Russo-Japanese Relations," *Comparative Strategy*, Vol. XIV, No. 1, 1993, pp. 173-198; Stephen Blank, "Diplomacy at an Impasse: Russia and Japan in a New Asia," *Korean Journal of Defense Analysis*, Vol. V, No. 1, Spring/Summer, 1993, pp. 141-164; "Voyennaya Doktrina, Rossiiskoi Federatsii-Proekt," *Krasnaya Zvezda*, October 9, 1999, pp. 3-4; Moscow, Russia, *Nezavisimoye Voyennoe Obozreniye*, January 14, 2000, *FBIS SOV*; Moscow, Russia, *Nezavisimaya Gazeta*, April 22, 2000, *FBIS SOV*, April 24, 2000; "Yeltsin Okays Russian Foreign Policy Concept," *Current Digest of the Post-Soviet Press* (CDPP), Vol. XLV, No. 17, May 26, 1993, p. 15; Evgeny Bazhanov, "Russian Perspectives on China's Foreign Policy and Military Development," Jonathan D. Pollack and Richard H. Yang, eds., *In China's Shadow: Regional Perspectives on Chinese Foreign Policy and Military Development*, Santa Monica, CA: Rand Corporation, 1998, pp. 71-76; Yuri S. Tsyganov, "Russia and China: What is in the Pipeline," in Gennady Chufrin, ed., *Russia and Asia: The Emerging Security Agenda*, Oxford, UK: Oxford University Press for SIPRI, 1999, pp. 301-303.

166. E. G., Vyacheslav Nikonov, "Putin's Strategy," *Nezavisimaya Gazeta*, December 22, 2004: Mikhail Margelov, "What Need Is There for the OSCE," Moscow, Russia, *Nezavisimaya Gazeta*, January 19, 2004, *FBIS SOV*; Address by Defense Minister Sergei Ivanov, "Russia's Armed Forces and Its Geopolitical Priorities," Moscow, *www.polit.ru*, February 3, 2004, *FBIS SOV*; Surkov.

167. Phillip Bobbitt, *The Shield of Achilles: War, Peace, and the Course of History*, New York: Alfred A. Knopf, 2002, pp. 634-638.

168. *Ibid*.

169. *Ibid*.

170. Sergei Lavrov, "Global Politics Needs Openness and Democracy," *Izvestiya*, in Russian, April 24, 2007, *FBIS SOV*.

171. Quoted in Michael Emerson, "From an Awkward Partnership to a Greater Europe: A European Perspective," Dana Allin and Michael H. Emerson, eds., *Readings in European Security*, Vol. III, Brussels, Belgium, and London, UK: Center for European Policy Studies and International Institute for Security Studies, 2005, p. 19.

172. Robert Legvold, ed., *Russian Foreign Policy in the 21st Century & the Shadow of the Past*, New York: Columbia University Press, 2007, is a recent exception to this trend.

173. Rieber, "Persistent Factors in Russian Foreign Policy: An Interpretation," p. 321.

174. Neuman Hausikala.

175. Iver Neumann.

176. Moscow, Russia, *Ekho Moskvy*, in Russian, February 17, 2007, Open Source Committee, *FBIS SOV*.

177. Yuri Ushakov, "From Russia With Like," *Los Angeles Times*, February 1, 2007, available from *www.latimes.com*.

178. Mehdiyeva, p. 24.

179. "Russia Ready to Cooperate With NATO on an Equal Basis Only-Foreign Ministry," Moscow, *Interfax*, in Russian, April 8, 2009, *FBIS SOV*.

180. Sergei Markedonov, "NATO's Anniversary Summit: the European Dimension," Moscow, *politkom.ru*, in Russian, April 6, 2009, *FBIS SOV*.

181. "Transcript: Sergei Ivanov," *Financial Times*, April 18, 2007, available from *www.ft.com/cms/s/b7e458ea-ede1-11db-8584-000b5df10621.html*.

182. Pipes; Lunacharsky's remarks cited in Ronald Hideo Hayashida, *The Third Front: The Politics of Soviet Mass Education 1917-1918*, Unpublished Ph.D. Dissertation, Columbia University, p. 148.

183. "Transcript: Sergei Ivanov."

184. "Putin Warns Russia Political Reform Needs Caution," *Radio Free Europe Radio Liberty*, January 22, 2010, available from *www.rferl.org*.

185. Tatiana Stoyanova, "Are 'They' the Main Threat to Russia?" Moscow, Russia, *politkom.ru*, in Russian, February 25, 2011, *FBIS SOV*.

186. Dmitri Trenin, "Building a Republic 20 Years After the Putsch," *Moscow Times*, August 16, 2011.

187. "Vladimir Shlapentokh, "Russian Intellectuals Hold the Russians in Contempt: Not Ready for Democracy," p. 41, available from *shlapentokh.wordpress.com*.

188. "'Sovereign Democracy' Intrinsically Russian-Speaker," *Interfax*, April 27, 2011, *Johnson's Russia List*, April 28, 2011.

189. Cited in Stephen White, *Understanding Russian Politics*, Cambridge, MA: Cambridge University Press, 2011, pp. 110-111.

190. Richard Pipes, *Russian Conservatism and Its Critics: A Study in Political Culture*, New Haven, CT: Yale University Press, 2007.

191. "Meeting on Preparations for Celebrating the 1150th Anniversary of Russia's Statehood," July 22, 2011, available from *eng. kremlin.ru/transcripts/2626.*

192. *Ibid.*

193. *Ibid.*

194. *Ibid.*

195. Vladimir Shlapentokh, "Are Today's Authoritarian Leaders Doomed to Be Indicted When They Leave Office? The Russian and Other Post-Soviet Cases," *Communist and Post-Communist Studies,* Vol. XXXIX, No. 2, Autumn, 2006, pp. 462-63.

196. Sergei Gavrov, "Is the Transition to Authoritarianism Irreversible?" *Russian Social Science Review*, Vol. XKVIII, No. 3, May-June, 2007, pp. 22-23.

197. Cited in Cathy Young, "From Russia With Loathing," *New York Times*, November 21, 2008, available from *www.nytimes. com.*

198. Fedor Lukyanov, "Political No-Road Map," Moscow, Russia, *Gazeta.ru*, in Russian, April 3, 2008, *FBIS SOV*; Tsypkin cites analogous examples of this, Tsypkin, pp. 784-787.

199. Fedor Lukyanov, "Russian Dilemmas in a Multipolar World," *Journal of International Affairs*, Vol. LXIII, No. 2, Spring/ Summer, 2010, p. 28.

200. Timofei Bordachev, "Multipolarity, Anarchy, and Security," in Ivan Krastev *et al., What Does Russia Think?* London, UK: European Council on Foreign Relations, 2009, p. 63, available from *www.ecfr.eu.*

201. Kari Roberts, "Jets, Flags, and a New Cold War?" *International Journal*, Vol. LXV, No. 4, Autumn, 2010, p. 962.

202. Vladimir Kara-Murza, "Stealing the Vote: the Kremlin Fixes Another Election," *World Affairs*, September-October, 2011, pp. 60-63.

203. Zoltan Barany, *Democratic Breakdown and the Decline of the Russian Military*, Princeton, NJ: Princeton University Press, 2007, pp. 167-168.

204. "Russia On the Brink of Civil War," Moscow, *Vlasti*, in Russian, April 19, 2009, *FBIS SOV*.

205. *Ibid.*

206. *Ibid.*

207. Iriana Borogan, "In Shoulder-Boards: The Kremlin's Anti-Crisis Project: When OMON Rushes to Help," Moscow, Russia, *Yezhenedevnyi Zhurnal*, in Russian, December 15, 2009, *FBIS SOV*.

208. Moscow, *Agentstvo Voyennykh Novostey Internet Version*, in Russian, July 4, 2008, *FBIS SOV*.

209. Sergei Karaganov, "The Unfinished Cold War," *The Jordan Times*, August 13, 2009, available from *www.jordantimes. com/?news=19064*.

210. Trenin is quoted in Sergei Strokan and Dmitry Sidorov, "In the World: and Now the Rest," Moscow, Russia, *Kommersant Online*, in Russian, July 27, 2009, *FBIS SOV*.

211. House of Commons Defence Committee, *Russia: A New Confrontation? Team Report of Session 2008-09*, London, UK: The Stationery House for the House of Commons, 2009, p. 56.

212. "Charlemagne, "Europe's Bear Problem," *The Economist*, February 27, 2010, p. 61.

213. Ulam, Kennan.

214. Rieber, ""Persistent Factors in Russian Foreign Policy: An Interpretation," pp. 315-359; Rieber, "How Persistent Are Persistent Factors?" pp. 205-277.

215. Oleg Shchedrov, "U.S. Uses Double Standards Over Protests: Russia."

216. *Reuters*, November 27, 2007; "Foreign Ministry: Russia Rules Out Double Standards," available from *en.civilg8.ru1779. php*. These are two typical examples where Russia accuses the West of applying double standards over human rights and civil rights violations in Russia and towards the liberalization of the EU's energy markets while demanding the same in Russia.

217. Moscow, Russia, *Vek* (Electronic Version), in Russian, November 26, 1999, *FBIS SOV*, for a justification of the Chechen offensive in terms of the domino theory, underscoring Putin's sense of the precariousness of state power in the provinces as for other Russian observers. See Vladimir Baranovsky, "Russia and Asia: Challenges and Opportunities for National and International Security," Gennady Chufrin, ed., *Russia and Asia: The Emerging Security Agenda*, Oxford, UK: Oxford University Press for the SIPRI Institute, 1999, p. 14.

218. Alexander Lukin, "Russia's China Card: Eyes on Washington," Byung-Kook Kim and Anthony Jones, eds., *Power and Security in Northeast Asia: Shifting Strategies*, Boulder, CO: Lynne Rienner Publishers, 2007, pp. 167-193; Rouben Azizian, "Russia and the Asia-Pacific: Trends, Threats, and Common Threads," and Artyom Lukin, "Regionalism in Northeast Asia and Prospects for Russia-U.S. Cooperation," both in Rouben Azizian, ed., *Russia and America in the Asia-Pacific*, Honolulu: HI: Asia-Pacific Center for Security Studies, 2007, pp. 16-36 and 227-230, respectively.

219. Moscow, *Nezavisimaya Gazeta Internet Version*, March 17, 2000, *FBIS SOV*; *FBIS SOV*, November 29, 1999; *ITAR-TASS*, March 1, 2000; *FBIS SOV*, March 1, 2000. Vladimir Putin, "Russia at the Turn of the Millennium," available from *www.geocities.com/ capitolhill/parliament/3005/poutine.html*.

220. *FBIS SOV*, November 29, 1999.

221. Moscow, Russia, *Nezavisimaya Gazeta*, (Electronic Version), March 17, 2000, *FBIS SOV*; Moscow, Russia, *Vek* (Electronic Version), November 26, 1999, *FBIS SOV*, November 29, 1999; Moscow, Russia, *ITAR-TASS*, March 1, 2000, *FBIS SOV*.

222. Vladimir Putin, "Russia at the Turn of the Millennium," available from *www.geocities.com/capitolhill/parliament/3005/poutine.html*.

223. "Putin says Russia can defend its interests at home and abroad," *RIA Novosti*, November 18, 2007; Vladimir Putin, "Meeting with Members of the Nakhimov and Suvorov Military Academies and Representatives of Youth Organizations After Laying Flowers at the Monument to Mini and Pozharskii," November 4, 2007, available from *www.kremlin.ru/eng/text/speeches/2007/11/04*. See the articles in the Russian Journal (English language version) *Military Thought*, No. 2, 2007, from speeches given at a conference at the Academy of Military Sciences in Moscow, January 20, 2007; M. A. Gareev, "Russia's New Military Doctrine: Structure and Substance," pp. 1-14; Y. N. Baluyevsky, "Theoretical and Methodological Foundations of the Military Doctrine of the Russian Federation (Plans for a Report), pp. 15-22; A. S. Rukshin, "Doctrinal Views on Employment and Organizational Development of the Armed Forces of Russia," pp. 23-30. Gareev is President of the Academy, Baluyevsky is Chief of Staff, and Rukshin his Deputy.

224. Heinrich Vogel, "How Not to Deal With a Backsliding Russia," *Internationale Politik*, Winter, 2005, p. 59.

225. Paul Goble, "Window on Eurasia: Russians See Themselves as Both 'the Greatest and Most Oppressed of Nations, Moscow Commentator Says," *Johnson's Russia List*, May 31, 2011.

226. "Russia At Risk of Collapsing, Putin Says," *Associated Press*, April 18, 2005, Retrieved from Lexis-Nexis; "Interview with Chief of the Presidential Staff Dmitri Medvedev," *Ekspert Weekly*, April 5, 2005, retrieved from Lexis-Nexis; "Vladislav Surkov's Secret Speech: How Russia Should Fight International Conspiracy," available from *www.mosnews.com*, July 12, 2005; "Interview with Vladislav Surkov, Moscow, Russia, *Ekho Moskvy, FBIS SOV*, September 29, 2004.

227. *Ibid.*; General M. A. Gareyev (Gareev), "Problems of Maintaining Defense Security in Today's World," *European Security*, Vol. X, No. 3, Autumn, 2001, pp. 36-37.

228. Baluyevsky, p. 17.

229. Gareev, pp. 4-5.

230. Western analysts have noted this as well. Jacob Kipp, "Russia: New Draft Military Doctrine," Ustina Markus and Daniel N. Nelson, eds., *Brassey's Eurasian and East European Security Yearbook*, Washington, DC: Brassey's, 2000, p. 343.

231. "Putin Interviewed by Journalists from G8 countries — text," June 4, 2007, available from *www.kremlin.ru*, Retrieved from Nexis-Lexis.

232. Moscow, *Ministry of Foreign Affairs Internet Version, "Russian President Addresses Munich Forum, Answers Questions on Iran,* February 12, 2007, *FBIS SOV*. The question and answer session from which these remarks are taken are not on the *kremlin.ru* website.

233. "Interview with General Yuri Baluyevsky, First Deputy Defense Minister and Chief of the Russian Federation Armed Forces General Staff, Moscow, Russia, *Rossiyskaya Gazeta,* February 21, 2007 *FBIS SOV*.

234. *FBIS SOV*, February 12, 2007; "Speech and the Following Discussion at the Munich Conference on Security," February 10, 2007.

235. Ellen Barry, "Putin Aide Says Foreign Hands Are Behind Protests," *New York Times*, February 4, 2012, available from *www. nytimes.com*; Thomas L. Friedman, "Russia: Sort of But Not Really," *New York Times*, February 5, 2012, available from *www. nytimes.com*.

236. Andrew Monaghan, "Medvedev's Modernization: Towards a Russian Strategy," Christopher M. Schaubelt, ed., *Towards a Comprehensive Approach: Strategic and Operational Challenges*, Rome, Italy: NATO Defense College, 2011, pp. 115-121.

237. Vladimir Isachenkov, "Putin Lashes Out at Political Enemies," *Associated Press*, December 2, 2007.

238. Mohammad Ayoob, "From Regional System to Regional Society: Exploring Key Variables in the Construction of Regional

Order," *Australian Journal of International Affairs*, Vol. LIII, No. 3, 1999, pp. 247-260; "Inequality and theorizing in International Relations: The Case for Subaltern Realism," *International Studies Review*, Vol. IV, No 3, 2002, pp. 127-148, and the works cited therein.

239. Mohammad Ayoob, "From Regional System to Regional Society: Exploring Key Variables in the Construction of Regional Order," *Australian Journal of International Affairs*, Vol. LIII, No. 3, 1999, pp. 247-260; Mohammad Ayoob, "Inequality and Theorizing in International Relations: The Case for Subaltern Realism," *International Studies Review*, Vol. IV, No. 3, 2002, pp. 127-148, and the works cited therein.

240. As quoted in Mikhail Alekseev, *Regionalism of Russia's Foreign Policy in the 1990s: A Case of "Reversed Anarchy,"* Donald W. Treadgold Papers, Seattle, WA: University of Washington, Henry M. Jackson School of International Studies, No. 37, 2003, p. 12.

241. Amitav Acharya, "Human Security and Asian Regionalism: A Strategy of Localization," Amtiav Acharya and Evelyn Goh, eds., *Reassessing Security Cooperation in the Asia-Pacific: Competition, Congruence, and Transformation*, Cambridge, MA: MIT Press, 2007, p. 241.

242. Cooper.

243. Stephen E. Hanson, "The Uncertain Future of Russia's Weak State Authoritarianism," *East European Politics and Societies*, Vol. XXI, No. 1, January, 2007, p. 69.

244. Timofei Bordachev, "Russia's Europe Dilemma: Democratic Partner vs. Authoritarian Satellite," Andrew Kuchins and Dmitri Trenin, eds., *Russia: The Next Ten Years, A Collection of Essays to Mark Ten Years of the Carnegie Moscow Center*, Moscow, Russia: Carnegie Center, 2004, p. 120.

245. Vladimir Mau, "The Role of the State and the Creation of a Market Economy in Russia," *BOFIT Discussion Papers*, No. 23, 2011.

246. Gordon M. Hahn, *Russia's Islamic Threat*, New Haven, CT, and London, UK: Yale University Press, 2007, p. 1.

247. Dov Lynch, "'The Enemy Is At the Gate': Russia After Beslan," *International Affairs*, Vol. LXXXI (1), 2005, pp. 141–161.

248. *Ibid.*

249. *Ibid.*; Vyacheslav Nikonov, "Putin's Strategy," *Nezavisimaya Gazeta*, December 22, 2004, Retrieved from Lexis-Nexis; "The People Said 'No', and That Started It: Aleksander Kwasniecki Talking to Warsaw's Polityka," *Transatlantic Internationale Politik*, No. 1, 2005, p. 64.

250. Sergey Kolmakov, "The Ukrainian Elections—Views From Russia *Access PBN*, Vol. I, No. 23, January 25, 2005; Nikonov.

251. *Current Digest of the Post-Soviet press* (Henceforth CDPP), Vol. LVI, No. 48, December 29, 2004, p. 10.

252. "Russia At Risk of Collapsing, Putin Says," *Associated Press*, April 18, 2005, Retrieved from Lexis-Nexis; "Interview with Chief of the Presidential Staff Dmitri Medvedev," *Ekspert Weekly*, April 5, 2005, retrieved from Lexis-Nexis; "Vladislav Surkov's Secret Speech: How Russia Should Fight International Conspiracy," July 12, 2005, available from *www.mosnews.com*; "Interview with Vladislav Surkov, Moscow, Russia, *Ekho Moskvy*, FBIS SOV, September 29, 2004.

253. Philip Hanson, "The Turn to Statism in Russian Economic Policy, *The International Spectator*, Vol. XLII, No. 1, March, 2007, pp. 54-55.

254. Yevgeny M. Primakov, *Gody v Bol'shoi Politike*, Moscow, Russia: Sovershenno Sekretno, 1999, pp. 133-135.

255. Vladimir Putin, "Speech at the Reception on the Occasion of National Unity Day," November 4, 2007, available from *www.kremlin.ru/eng/text/speeches/2007/11/04*.

256. General M.A. Gareyev (Gareev), "Problems of Maintaining Defense Security, in Today's World," *European Security*, Vol. X, No. 3, Autumn 2001, pp. 36-37.

257. John Loewenhardt, "Russia and Europe: Growing Apart Together," *Brown Journal of World Affairs*, Vol. VII, No. 1, Winter-Spring 2000, p. 171.

258. Putin so likes this poem that he quotes it to foreign visitors, e.g., French President Sarkozy, October 2007, "France's Nicolas Sarkozy Finally Finds Someone to Admire—Putin and Russia," October 10, 2007, *www.pravda.ru*.

259. Putin, "Russia at the Turn of the Millennium"; "Interview With Foreign Minister Yevgeny Primakov," Moscow, Russia, *Rossiyskaya Gazeta*, in Russian, December 17, 1996, *FBIS SOV*.

260. *Ibid.*

261. Dmitri Trenin, "Russia Leaves the West," *Foreign Affairs*, Vol. LXXXV, No. 4, July-August 2006, pp. 85-96.

262. Stanislav Secrieriu, "Russia's Foreign Policy Under Putin: 'CIS Project' Renewed," *UNISCI Discussion Papers*, No. 10, January 2006, p. 291.

263. Trenin, "Russia Leaves the West," pp. 85-96.

264. Maura Reynolds, "Moscow Has Chechnya Back—Now What?" *Los Angeles Times*, June 19, 2000.

265. Quoted in Boris Rumer, "Central Asia: At the End of the Transition," Boris Rumer, ed., *Central Asia At the End of Transition*, Armonk, NY: M. E. Sharpe & Co. Inc., 2005, p. 47.

266. Quoted in Michael Emerson, "From an Awkward Partnership to a Greater Europe: A European Perspective," Dana Allin and Michael H. Emerson, eds., *Readings in European Security*, Vol. III, Brussels, Belgium, and London, UK: Center for European Policy Studies and International Institute for Security Studies, 2005, p. 19.

267. E.g., Alexei Pushkov, "Quo Vadis? Scenarios for Russia," *International Affairs*, No. 3, 2002, p. 71.

268. Julie Wilhelmsen and Geir Flikke, "Evidence of Russia's Bush Doctrine in the CIS," *European Security*, Vol. XIV, No. 3, September, 2005, pp. 387-417.

269. Sergei Lavrov, "Vneshnepoliticheskaya Samostoyatel' nost' Rossii Bezuslovnyi Imperativ" ("Russia's Foreign Policy Autonomy is an Unconditional Imperative"), *Moskovskiye Novosti*, January 19, 2007, available from *www.mn.ru/issue.php?2007-1-56*; Gareyev, "Russia New Military Doctrine: Structure, Substance," p. 4.

270. Cited in Geoffrey Roberts, *Stalin's Wars: From World Wars to Cold Wars, 1939-1953*, New Haven, CT, and London, UK: Yale University Press, 2007, p. 22.

271. Reynolds, "Moscow Has Chechnya Back—Now What?"

272. Quoted in Rumer, "Central Asia: At the End of the Transition," p. 47.

273. Cited in Yegor Gaidar, *Collapse of an Empire: Lessons for Modern Russia*, Antonia Bouis, trans., Washington, DC: Carnegie Endowment for International Peace, 2007, p. x.

274. *Ibid.*, pp. ix-xviii.

275. Dietrich Geyer, *Russian Imperialism: The Interaction of Domestic and Foreign Policy, 1860-1914*, Bruce Little, trans., New Haven, CT, and London, UK: Yale University Press, 1987, p. 64.

276. *Ibid.*, pp. 1-123.

277. Larissa Zakharova, "Autocracy and the Reforms of 1861-1874 in Russia: Choosing Paths of Development," Daniel Field, trans., Ben Eklof, John Bushnell, and Larissa Zakharaova, eds. *Russia's Great Reforms, 1855-1881*, Bloomington, IN: Indiana University Press, 1994, pp. 19-39.

278. Theodore Taranovski, ed., *Reform in Modern Russian History: Progress or Cycle?* Washington, DC and Cambridge, UK: Woodrow Wilson Center Press and Cambridge University Press, 1995.

279. E.g., V. Kuznechevsky, "Russia-EU Samara Summit," *International Affairs* (Moscow) No. 4, 2007, pp. 84-86. Since this journal is the journal of the Ministry of Foreign Affairs, this viewpoint's frequent appearance there is, to use a Soviet neologism, no accident.

280. Hence the official promotion of Russian Orthodoxy as a state religion and the promotion of an ideology that is not far removed from Nicholas I's official nationality of autocracy, orthodoxy, and nationality (i.e., Russianness).

281. Nicholas Riasanaovsky, *Nicholas I and Official Nationality in Russia, 1825-1855,* Berkeley and Los Angeles, CA: University of California Press, 1969; W. Bruce Lincoln, *Nicholas I: Emperor and Autocrat of All the Russias,* Dekalb, IL, Northern Illinois University Press, 1989.

282. Chaykovskaya.

283. *Interfax Russia & CIS Presidential Bulletin Report,* July 13, 2007, Open Source Committee, *FBIS SOV,* July 13, 2007.

284. Dale R. Herspring, "Putin and the Reemergence of the Russian Military," *Problems of Post-Communism,* Vol. LIV, No. 1, January-February, 2007, p. 24.

285. Dmitri Trenin, "Putin's Choice, " *The Economist,* December 4, 2006, available from *www.economist.com.index.html*; Dmitri Trenin, *Getting Russia Right,* Washington, DC: Carnegie Endowment for International Peace, 2007; Lilia Shevtsova, *Russia - Lost in Transition: The Yeltsin and Putin Legacies* (Paperback), Arch Tait, trans., Washington, DC: 2007.

286. Interview With Director General of the Political Technologies Center, Igor Bunin, *Ezhednevnaya Gazeta,* March 26, 2004, available from *www.fednews.ru*.

287. Michael McFaul and Katherine Stoner-Weiss, "The Myth of the Authoritarian Model: How Putin's Crackdown Holds Russia Back," *Foreign Affairs,* January/February 2008, available from *carnegieendowment.org/2008/01/01/myth-of-authoritarian-model-how-putin-s-crackdown-holds-russia-back/qwb*.

288. Taylor, *Russia's Power Ministries: Coercion and Commerce*, Syracuse, NY: Institute for National Security and Counterterrorism, Syracuse University, 2007, and his Presentation at the Carnegie Endowment for International Peace on the Russian Power Structures, November 9, 2007.

289. Lincoln; Bunin, Interview; Peter Baker and Susan Glasser, *Kremlin Rising: Vladimir Putin's Russia and the End of Revolution*, New York : Scribner's, 2005, p. 417; Steven Rosefielde, *Russia in the 21st Century: the Prodigal Superpower*, Cambridge, MA: Cambridge University Press, 2004; Marshall T. Poe, *The Russian Moment in World History*, Princeton, NJ: Princeton University Press, 2003; Stefan Hedlund, *Russian Path Dependence*, London, UK: Routledge, 2005; Emil Pain, "Will Russia Transform Into a Nationalist Empire," *Russia in Global Affairs*, Vol. III, No. 2, April-June, 2005, pp. 71-80.

290. Francesca Mereu, "Putin's Campaign has Kiev on Edge," *Moscow Times.com*, October 28, 2004, available from *www.moscowtimes.com/stories/2004/10/28/001.html*.

291. Trenin, *Getting Russia Right*; Shevtsova, *Russia — Lost in Transition*.

292. Zakharova, pp. 19-39.

293. Dmitri Trenin and Bobo Lo, "The Landscape of Russian Foreign Policy Decision-Making," Moscow, Russia: Moscow Center of the Carnegie Endowment for International Peace, 2005, p. 9.

294 . Pierre Hassner, "Russia's Transition to Autocracy," *Journal of Democracy*, Vol. XIX, No. 2, April, 2008, pp. 13-15, makes this point why the appearance of great power status is crucial to the regime's domestic standing.

295. Julie Wilhelmsen and Geir Flikke, "Copy that — A Russian 'Bush Doctrine' in the CIS?" Oslo, Norway: Norwegian Institute of International Affairs, 2005, Yevgeny Primakov, *Russian Crossroads: Toward the New Millennium*, New Haven, CT, and London, UK: Yale University Press, 2004, p. 11.

296. Stephen Blank, "Military Threats and Threat Assessment in Russia's New Defense Doctrine and Security Concept," Michael H. Crutcher, ed., *The Russian Armed Forces at the Dawn of the Millennium,* Carlisle Barracks, PA: Center for Strategic Leadership, U.S. Army War College, 2001, pp. 191-220; also published as, "Military Threats and Threat Assessment in Russia's New Defense Doctrine and Security Concept," *Treadgold Papers,* No. 31, Seattle, WA: University of Washington Press, 2001.

297. Lincoln, and here one may simply cite the many references to the power vertical made by Putin and his subordinates, and which are found throughout the media from 2000 on. See also Shevtsova, *Putin's Russia,* Revised and Expanded Ed., Antonia W. Bouis, trans., Washington, DC, 2005.

298. *Ibid.*

299. Hellie, "The Structure of Russian Imperial History," pp. 88-112; Baker and Glasser, *Kremlin Rising,* p. 417; Rosefielde, *Russia in the 21st Century;* Poe, *The Russian Moment in World History;* Hedlund, *Russian Path Dependence;* Pain, "Will Russia Transform Into a Nationalist Empire," pp. 71-80; Kotkin, "It's Gogol Again"; Pipes, *Russia Under the Old Regime;* Blank, *Rosoboroneksport;* Balzer, "Confronting the Global Economy After Communism: Russia and China Compared."

300. Alexander Golts and Tonya Putnam, "State Militarism and Its Legacies: Why Military Reform Has Failed in Russia," *International Security,* Vol. XXIX, No. 2, Fall 2004, pp. 121-159; Aleksandr' Golts, *Armiya Rossii: 11 Poteryannykh Let,* Moscow, Russia: Zakharov, 2004. ▸

301. Wallander, Testimony.

302. *FBIS SOV,* November 29, 1999, Baranovsky, p. 14.

303. Stephen Blank, "Diplomacy at an Impasse: Russia and Japan in a New Asia," *Korean Journal of Defense Analysis,* Vol. V, No. 1, Spring/Summer 1993, pp. 141-164.

304. *Ibid.*

305. Robert O. Freedman, "Russia and Central Asia Under Yeltsin," available from *www.acdis.uiuc.edu/Research/S&Ps/1996-1997/S&P_X/Freedman.htm.*

306. Stephen Blank, "From Kosovo to Kursk: Russian Defense Policy From Yeltsin to Putin," *Korean Journal of Defense Analysis,* Vol. XII, No. 2, Winter, 2000, pp. 231-273; Talbott.

307. Blank, "Diplomacy at an Impasse: Russia and Japan in a New Asia," pp. 141-164.

308. Talbott, Petro, p. 47.

309. "Kontseptsiya Vneshnei Politiki (1993) Rossiiskoi Federatsii" Special Issue of *Diplomaticheskii Vestnik,* January 1993, pp. 3-23.

CHAPTER 3

IDEOLOGY AND SOFT POWER IN CONTEMPORARY RUSSIA

Ariel Cohen

Since the Soviet era, Russia has viewed soft power as a tool of statecraft, from a leaflet to a mob slogan to ideology, just like a progression from a gun to a nuclear weapon. The Russian leadership views its ability to use soft power as similar to its use during the Cold War: To extend its influence and to constrain U.S. policy. While in the 21st century the methods Russia has at its disposal to hamper U.S. foreign policy and to change world opinion against the United States have changed, the end goal has not.

The Soviet Union was a highly ideological power. It amassed an enormous arsenal of print publications, movies, television and radio programming, and education exchange programs to promote further the Soviet message for communism and against the West. It had tens of thousands of leftist intellectuals at its disposal worldwide. These lessons are still informing today's Russian leadership.

Since then-president Vladimir Putin secured control of the media and political system in Russia in the last decade, his government has embarked on a quest for the hearts and minds of those outside Russia. This is where soft power is preferable to military ("hard") power in accomplishing state goals. Today, Russia's soft power is in the process of reestablishing itself as a regional and eventually worldwide force to promote Russia's interests, including by attacking America's global reputation.

RUSSIAN IDEOLOGICAL REINVIGORATION

Since the fall of the Soviet Union and the collapse of Marxist-Leninist (communist) single-track political philosophy, Russia has witnessed the growth of a myriad of divergent political perspectives. The Russian Constitution bans any particular ideology from being "official." As much as this pluralism has allowed many viewpoints, which previously would have been suppressed, to flourish, the most prominent contemporary philosophical and ideological trends have often been statist and nationalistic. Experts point out, without rancor, that the Putin reign is reminiscent of Emperor Nicholas I (1825-55).[1] Lately, these philosophies are informing the Kremlin's post-Soviet grand strategy.

Starting in the mid-1990s, then-Russian Foreign Minister Yevgeny Primakov began a new rapprochement with the emerging non-Western powers such as China, India, Iran, and the Muslim world in order to undermine the unipolar preeminence of Western Europe and the United States. While the world wanted to believe that Russia was no longer its legal predecessor, the Union of Soviet Socialist Republics (USSR), and abandoned forever its zero-sum world view, Primakov was engineering Russian foreign policy in order to prevent the rise of a unipolar world in which the United States was the sole superpower. He insisted that the post-Cold War world contained many power "poles," including the United States, Russia with its surrounding sphere of influence, the European Union (EU), China, and Latin America.[2] Through this time, Russia was building the relationships beyond the Western alliances that would become the driving forces to reduce American power in the 1990s.

In the aftermath of the Soviet collapse, the Russian public opinion and emerging civil society held mostly positive feelings toward the United States and the West. However, "shame, blame, and nostalgia" began to percolate through society as the country defaulted on its bonds in 1998, and the architect of friendship with the West, President Boris Yeltsin, was deeply unpopular.[3]

In order to spread a coherent message of Russian retrenchment against the West, Putin and his government must find and implement a directive at home and would project it abroad. One element of this was his famous dictum that the collapse of the Soviet Union was the greatest geopolitical catastrophe of the 20th century. This means that the search for the new iteration of the Soviet global power, and its imperial posture in Eurasia and Eastern Europe, are goals to strive for.

In that respect, it is instructive to examine the evolution of the changing philosophy of Russian political analyst, Fyodor Lukyanov. Affiliated with a prominent foreign-relations Moscow think tank, the Council on Foreign and Defense Politics, Lukyanov was once a leading liberal supporter of better relations between Russia and the United States. Over time, Lukyanov began to criticize the allegedly domineering "American Empire," stating that "in the foreseeable future, a new world architecture will be designed according to American patterns."[4]

More extreme political philosophers like Alexander Dugin evolved, combining in their outlook the Neo-Nazi, European New Right, and Russian imperialist and Christian Orthodox perspectives. Dugin vouches for an imperialist Eurasianist foreign policy that centered on expanding Russian influence throughout former Soviet satellites by using tools such as the Orthodox Church, media outreach, and "the manipulation of information by the secret services."[5]

In 2008, Professor Igor Panarin, a Russian Secret Police (KGB) veteran and a political analyst who advises the Federation Council, the upper house of the Russian Parliament, has predicted the imminent demise of the United States by 2010. Panarin stated that this prediction "reflects a very pronounced degree of anti-Americanism in Russia today" that is "much stronger than it was in the Soviet Union."[6] Propagandists like Dugin and Panarin are close to the Russian military, intelligence community, and generally, the ruling classes within Russia. Clearly, their services are in demand.

Vladimir Putin himself has articulated a foreign policy view that includes a sphere of influence for Russia; the vision of the Eurasian Union; protection and expansion of the Russian language and Russian Orthodox (Moscow Patriarchy rite) religion; use of energy and economic power as primary geopolitical tools; and neutralizing foreign, especially Western, powers, attempting to act in the former Soviet areas.

RUSSIA'S SOFT POWER TOOLS IN MEDIA

With the increased control over the most popular print, radio, and television outlets in Russia, the Kremlin is now able to project not only a unified, patriotic image of Russia abroad but also to promote the idea of a multipolar world. At the core of Russia's multipolar vision is the hostile message that U.S. dominance must be weakened and the influence of Russia and other opponents of the United States, such as China, Iran, and Venezuela, must be expanded. Therefore, any Russian use of public diplomacy or strategic communication must be anti-American by nature.

Russia's premier soft power instrument is its bur-
geoning global television empire, led by its flagship
news network RT. Formerly known as Russia Today,
RT was launched in 2005 with the stated objective to
"improve Russia's image around the world" in the
face of the alleged anti-Russian bias from outlets like
Cable News Network (CNN) and British Broadcasting
Company (BBC). Although occasionally giving view-
ers a more positive perspective of Russia, the vast majority of RT's content is aimed directly at criticizing
the United States, Western Europe, the North Atlantic
Treaty Organization (NATO), and the global economic order, including avidly glorifying the "Occupy Wall
Street" protests. Suffice to say that America-hater and
convicted criminal, Lyndon La Rouche, is often interviewed by RT and other Russian TV channels as a
credible commentator. Moreover, RT is now unabash-
edly pro-Obama and anti-Republican, which raises
questions about its—and Russia's—intra-American
political agenda. The channel has received global con-
demnation for airing controversial programming such
as a documentary that claims that the September 11,
2001 (9/11) terrorist attacks were committed by the
United States itself, not by Islamist terrorists.[7]

RT's apparatus includes three separate satellite
channels, which are available as cable channels in
Washington, DC, in English, Spanish, and Arabic; a
website with live streams of the channels; a Twitter
feed; and a popular YouTube Channel with over 200
million hits.[8] Virtually all of RT's content is available
for free.

The budgets of all of these Russian-based global
news outlets have grown significantly since the early
2000s, and with the help of the Internet, all of Russia's outlets can reach people all around the world.

For example, RT's budget has grown from $30 million to around $150 million in 2008.[9] Experts believe RT now has a budget in excess of $200 million. As oil revenues increase, these and other media budgets will only grow.

RT even showcases useful American citizens who have become champions against the U.S. Government, using Russian media outlets to spread their message. For example, former U.S. Marine and political commentator Adam Kokesh was the host of his own program on the popular Russian news channel RT. According to Accuracy in Media, RT exploits Americans like Kokesh to parrot Russian agitprop against the United States. Another American commentator and radio talk-show host, Alex Jones, frequently appears on RT to condemn American domestic and foreign policy, including America's support of Georgia during the 2008 Russian-Georgian War, calling the initial moments of the war a "sneak attack" by the American military-industrial complex against Russia.[10] Accuracy in Media states that to fulfill objectives of Russian propaganda, the country prefers "to use foreigners, especially Americans to make [Russia's] propaganda points."[11]

According to RT's website, RT has become one of the most watched global news channels in many major world cities, including Washington and New York.[12] The network was nominated for the best documentary prize from the 2011 Monte Carlo TV Festival and has received other worldwide acclaim that has raised RT's reputation.[13] Yet, the crude propagandistic tone of RT puts it behind France 24 and Deutsche Welle, let alone the dynamic Al Jazeera English and BBC.

Beyond the Internet, Russian based media is readily accessible in the West through cable and broadcast

TV, terrestrial radio, and national newspapers. As RT attempts to reach out with its anti-American agenda-driven news and commentary, Russia will continue to be able to guide and to distort the opinions of many North and Latin Americans, Europeans, Middle Easterners, and others.

Besides RT, the global Russian media is more balanced. It broadcasts through a global radio network called "The Voice of Russia" that goes back to Radio Comintern (Communist International) and is accessible on the Internet. "The Voice of Russia" is broadcast in many languages including English, Russian, French, Arabic, Spanish, German, and Chinese; and the radio network's website is available in these and other languages. Russia also takes advantage of Western print media by paying major European and American newspapers to have "Russia's side" appear in special advertising sections, entitled as *Russia Behind the Headlines* or *Russia Now,* that resemble articles written by the original newspaper.

The Russian base for much of Russia's global media is the Russian press agency *RIA Novosti,* capably led by its Director General, Svetlana Mironyuk. Whereas during the Soviet era *RIA Novosti* often was a cover for clandestine activities, today it mainly sticks to the official business. Unlike Associated Press or Reuters, *RIA Novosti* is state-owned. It is a professional source of news and information for Russian news outlets and international news organizations covering events in Russia. Recently, the agency has increased its presence beyond Russia by covering global events without the assistance of non-Russian news agencies.

RUSSIAN SOFT POWER AND THE RUSSIAN DIASPORA

Beyond what Russian state media broadcast for domestic and global consumption, Russian speakers and former Soviet citizens living outside Russia are increasingly becoming a target for the long arm of the Russian state. For the first time since the collapse of the Soviet Union, Russia's diaspora is no longer seen as hostile and anti-communist. On the contrary, the home country would like to curry favor with emigrants and not to lose it in favor of their new home.

Adopted in 1999, the Russia's "State Policy toward Compatriots Living Abroad" was updated in 2010 and now requires Russian compatriots to be "certified by a respective civil society organization or by the person's activities to promote and preserve the Russian language and culture."[14] In part through this "compatriots' policy," Russian soft power towards its diaspora is conducted through embassies, a network of establishments that promote Russian policy outlook, language, and culture under such banners as the Institute for Democracy and Cooperation, Russki Dom (Russia House), Russki Mir (Russian World), and online. However, some experts caution that these means of connecting Russian expats to their home country may have turned into bases for Russian intelligence operations and have certainly become advocates of Kremlin policies.

After the fall of the Soviet Union, the Russian government established Russia House, a network of over 50 global "Russophone centers" to promote Russian culture, Russian language and "ethnic identity" as well as to generate dialogue between Russians abroad and their "historical motherland."[15] Experts state that the budget for Russia House has swelled from $26 to 30 million, and plans are to expand the operation to 100 branches worldwide by 2020.[16]

Besides Russia House, Russian World is the Russian government's primary organization devoted to connecting to its diaspora through a "common bond between Russia and its emigrants who left" that would use the Russian language as the factor that bonds the two together.[17] Although initially nongovernmental, it quickly became absorbed into the propaganda and, apparently, the intelligence realms. According to the Estonian Security Police (KAPO), former Soviet intelligence teams "are active" within Estonia through Russian World, which some believe that this signals that Russian outreach organizations are serving "to advance Russia's foreign policy interests in the Baltics."[18]

Some analysts pointed to the use of the Russian Orthodox Church (Moscow Patriarchy) branches overseas as a conduit to the extensive governmental funding and influence. Just like Russian World, it is attempting to encourage expatriate Russians to "act" more Russian while living abroad. It also is trying to discourage emigrants from adopting the cultural mores, language, and political beliefs of their host country.[19] In fact, in 2006, Metropolitan Kirill, before he became the Patriarch of the Russian Orthodox Church, stated that Russians all over the world "should oppose Western civilization in its assertion of the universality of the Western tradition."[20] This typifies Russia's "compatriots' policy" that serves to keep Russian expatriates under its influence.

Finally, social networking is still one of the freest modes of exchange between Russia and the outside world. However, the Russian language social media are monitored and manipulated through dedicated interference (see below), though without the censorship that other media have. Additionally, organizations that track global Internet freedom have seen a growing intimidation from the government to those who disseminate information against the Kremlin.[21]

Recently, pro-Kremlin actors have found ways to undermine the legitimacy of these websites through acts of sabotage. One main form of sabotage is through intentional acts of incitement, known as "trolling," in which a specially trained user will intentionally publish inflammatory, libelous, or outlandish statements in order to evoke emotional responses from other users. This is done in order to derail or squash a legitimate debate, or spread chaos.

RUSSIAN USE OF "AGENTS OF INFLUENCE"

The use of "agents of influence" by Russia is quite prolific even after the end of the Cold War, as this has been a tried-and-true espionage tool going all the way back to the czarist intelligence services. They have become immersed in the centers of policy promotion, business, lobbying, and journalism to shape policy and American opinion to favor Russian interests. Russia's agents of influence have become an integral part of its campaign to increase Russia's influence in international affairs by weakening America's role in the world.

Targeting American domestic affairs has been one of Russia's greatest foreign priorities despite the collapse of the Soviet Union and the more cooperative relationship between Yeltsin's Russia and the United States. In his book, *Foundations of Geopolitics*, Dugin proposed that post-Soviet Russia should use Russian intelligence officers "to provoke all forms of instability and separatism" in the United States. He recommended agents achieve domestic instability by fomenting racial tensions, promoting "isolationist tendencies," and "actively supporting all dissident movements."[22]

A KGB defector alleged that The Russian Orthodox Church Outside of Russia (ROCOR) has become a main vehicle by which Russian intelligence agents penetrate into America through its unwary Russian-expat followers. According to former KGB officer Konstantin Preobrazhensky, once Russian Foreign Intelligence Service (SVR) agents entrench themselves into the Russian Orthodox Church in America, it becomes a "stronghold for Russian intelligence."[23] Subverted Russian churches in America can potentially become prime locations for subversive operations and for recruiting future Russian agents of influence in America. These allegations, which come from a single source interested in promoting his book, need further investigation. Yet, Russian intelligence services have amassed their own "'PR line officers," who work undercover as diplomats or journalists. They attempt to gain sensitive information, using their secret agents, contacts in the diplomatic sphere or within the American media, or plant rumors and misinformation.[24]

The high profile arrest in 2010 of a Russian spy ring that included Anna Kushchenko, also known as Anna Chapman, raised many questions with regards to Russian long-term intelligence goals in America, including the influence of the policy process. Developing intelligence assets for future insertion into the media process is a sophisticated use of soft power.

According to a Russian-born Canadian/American journalist Jamie Glazov, one of the stated goals of this failed spy ring was "to search and develop ties in policymaking circles in [the United States]." Some of the policy issues the spy ring tried to influence included nuclear weapons, U.S. arms control, Iran, Central Intelligence Agency (CIA) leadership, Congress, presidential elections, and political parties. One of the spy rings contacts included a New York "financier who was active in politics."[25] Fortunately, this group of failed spies did not manage to compromise the integrity of American foreign policy or national security, but this is only one of many examples of Russia's continued determination.

Another recently prominent case involved an exposed Russian alleged spy within the British Parliament. Katia Zatuliveter, an assistant for Mike Hancock, a member of the defense committee of the House of Commons, was arrested for spying on Hancock for the Russian SVR. Many believe that Zatuliveter intentionally targeted the powerful Member of Parliament (MP) as he is known as the "most pro-Russian MP from among all the countries of western Europe." It has been alleged that while Zatuliveter was working in Hancock's parliamentary office, the office sent requests for an "inventory of Britain's nuclear weapons arsenal" and "details of nuclear material outside international safeguards."[26] However, the pro-Russian statements of Mr. Hancock in the media represented a considerable boon for this alleged intelligence operation.

Russian firms, especially Gazprom, and the Russian government have spent millions of dollars on lobbyists to purvey their message and to influence politicians in Washington to influence policy. According to the Foreign Agents Registration Act (FARA) of the Department of Justice's second semi-annual report to Congress in 2010, Gazprom, Ketchum Inc., Techsnabexport, the St. Petersburg city government, and the Russian federal government have called upon the services of American lobbyists to influence policy and politicians.[27]

EXAMPLES OF RUSSIAN SOFT POWER IN ACTION: UKRAINE AND GEORGIA

Russia's soft power machine was put into practice first in its "near abroad," when major crises were unfolding that were threatening Russia's tenuous control over its "sphere of privileged interests." The foremost tests for determining the effectiveness of Russian soft power occurred in Ukraine and in Georgia.

The Kremlin has been active in its campaign to weaken pro-Russian political forces in Ukraine since the Kuchma presidency; however, the 2004 election and the Orange Revolution saw an onslaught of Russian TV agitprop towards opposition leaders Victor Yushchenko and Yulia Timoshenko and their supporters. The main focus of Russia's soft-power sabotage was primarily on ethnic tension and Eastern Ukrainians' loyalty to Russia, its culture, and language. The Fund for Effective Politics (FEP), directed by Gleb Pavlovsky, a "political technologist" and then-adviser to Putin, was one of the main bases for spreading misinformation on the Orange Revolution and attempts to discredit it through anti-American propaganda not seen since the height of the Cold War.[28] This included allegations of Mrs. Yushchenko, an American citizen, being a CIA agent and of clandestine funding of the "orange" forces.

Georgia has remained under the direction of pro-Western political forces led by Mikheil Saakashvili, in spite of heavy Russian interference in the country's affairs. Beyond the use of force in the 2008 Russian-Georgian war, Russian intrusion in Georgian politics has been steadfast and aggressive, including Russian-backed mass protests for Saakashvili's ouster and funding for some opposition politicians. From the aftermath of the 2008 Russian-Georgian war, Russia spread allegations that a tiny Georgia somehow endangered Russian sovereignty, or had committed "genocide" against South Ossetians, of which international observers have not found any evidence.

HOW THE UNITED STATES SHOULD RESPOND TO RUSSIAN SOFT POWER

The lessons from these two cases show how Russian soft power is a clear national security concern and can undermine domestic security and global stability. Therefore, the United States must formulate a clear and active strategy to combat Russian soft power operations within the United States and within its allies in order to protect national and global security.

The United States has fallen behind Russia in the struggle for hearts and minds through traditional and new forms of media. Through outlets like RT or on the Internet, Russia has already spread its message effectively by using these low-cost outreach tools, which connect millions instantaneously everywhere.[29] The United States must seize the opportunity to reach hundreds of millions of new audiences and those with whom the United States had lost touch after the end of the Cold War by increased use of low-cost new media on the Internet and mobile devices. Through these reinvigorated outreach efforts, the United States can effectively compete with Russian soft power to refute Russian distortions.

In using new technologies or other means to reach more audiences, the United States must remember how it engaged with its audience during the Cold War. Then the United States effectively promoted dialogue and exchanged ideas with foreign audiences, cultivated institutional relationships, assisting the education of future democratic leaders. Learning how the United States defeated Soviet soft power will help guide U.S. policy to combat Russian soft power. [30]

The U.S. Government, traditional media, and the public often view "new media" as a magic tool, portending a revolution in the way the U.S. Government conducts public diplomacy and addresses the world.[31] New media has shown itself to be the "game changer" that as of July 8, 2001, as former Undersecretary of State of Public Diplomacy and Public Affairs Judith McHale discussed in her confirmation hearing, can revolutionize how media communicates with its audience:

> [New media provides] the opportunity to move from an old paradigm, in which our government speaks as one to many, to a new model of engaging interactively and collaboratively across lines that might otherwise divide us from people around the world.[32]

In developing its ability to use "new media," the United States needs to establish a National Communications Strategy outlined by the Undersecretary of State for Public Diplomacy in order to organize one unified message against Russian soft power that is clear, concise, and believable. This National Communications Strategy should especially ensure that its message through new media is unique and identifiable from potential acts of informational sabotage, like trolling, and that it is disseminated through those outlets that access the most valuable audiences, such as young people and politically active groups. One way to promote the success of the U.S. informational campaign is to establish a research body to analyze how to best reach targeted audiences with which Russia has actively engaged.[33]

The United States must also continue to fund and to promote traditional forms of communication through outlets such as Radio Free Europe/Radio Liberty (RFE/RL), the Voice of America (VOA), and the publication of books and journals that comprise collaboration among Americans and talented locals, similar to RT recruiting British and American journalists and commentators to spread its message, to generate the most effective message for local audiences. In addition to its efforts abroad, the United States must improve its ability to counteract Russian information operations within the country, including within the Russian Orthodox Church in America, *Russki Mir*, and other Russian-led outlets.

The United States must carefully examine the scope and success of Russian informational operations. It must counteract Russian soft-power operations by directly engaging with the Russian-speaking diaspora and other groups targeted by Russian outreach programs. Furthermore, the United States must focus its most intense public diplomacy efforts on the former Soviet-controlled regions of Eastern and Central Europe. Although much of this region has become more economically and politically free and more integrated with the "Euro-Atlantic sphere," the United States must work with its allies in Europe to ensure that Russia does not corral this area back into its ideology sphere of influence and under its control.[34]

CONCLUSION

With the growth of Russian soft power on the Internet, through TV and other traditional media, and through government-sponsored expat organizations, the world is exposed to Russia's influence. In addition, the growing Russian outreach institutions, including the Russian Orthodox Church, which reach out to Russians and non-Russians abroad, have become the advocates and influencers for Russian policy abroad. Behind the glamor and the ostensibly innocuous nature of the Russian soft power, its goal is to strengthen Russia's international influence by weakening America's global leadership role.

Without a way to counteract this increasingly popular and effective media empire, the United States will continue to suffer damage to its interests abroad. Vladimir Lenin once said that "a lie told often enough becomes truth." Today, as before, the key to U.S. victory in the battle of ideas will be leadership and commitment to promote America's ideals to the world and to respond effectively to misinformation from Russian media.

ENDNOTES - CHAPTER 3

1. Artemii Yermakov, "Sovremennaya gosudarstvennaya idelologiya Rossii i ee 'nikolayevskie' korni" ("Contemporary state ideology in Russia and its 'Nicholaevan' roots") September 7, 2011, available from *samoderjavie.ru/node/328*.

2. Ariel Cohen, "The 'Primakov Doctrine': Russia's Zero-Sum Game with the United States," Washington, DC: The Heritage Foundation F.Y.I., No. 167, December 15, 1997, p. 3, available from *s3.amazonaws.com/thf_media/1997/pdf/fyi167.pdf*.

3. Ariel Cohen and Helle Dale, "Russian Anti-Americanism: A Priority Target for U.S.-Public Diplomacy," *The Heritage Foundation Backgrounder*, No. 2373, February 24, 2010, p. 2, available from *www.heritage.org/Research/Reports/2010/02/Russian-Anti-Americanism-A-Priority-Target-for-US-Public-Diplomacy.*

4. Fyodor Lukyanov, "Pax Americana: imperia obustraivaet mir," *Gazeta.ru*, April 4, 2003, available from *www.gazeta.ru/comments/2003/04/22108.shtml.*

5. Cohen and Dale, "Russian Anti-Americanism: A Priority Target for U.S.-Public Diplomacy," p. 5.

6. Andrew Osborn, "As if things weren't bad enough, Russian professor predicts end of U.S.," *Wall Street Journal*, December 29, 2008, available from *online.wsj.com/article/SB123051100709638419.html.*

7. *RT.com*, "Who was involved in 9/11? Documentary reveals shocking facts," September 11, 2008, available from *rt.com/news/who-was-involved-in-911-documentary-reveals-shocking-facts/.*

8. *RT.com*, "RT hits 200 million on Youtube," December 23, 2010, available from *rt.com/about/pressoffice/rt-hits-200-million-youtube/.*

9. Nikolaus von Twickel, "Russia Today courts views with controversy," *The Moscow Times*, March 23, 2010, available from *www.themoscowtimes.com/news/article/russia-today-courts-viewers-with-controversy/401888.html.*

10. "Alex Jones on Russia Today TV," *YouTube* (content from *Russia Today*), August 26, 2008, available from *www.youtube.com/watch?v=XcO8OBVCdCM*, September 20, 2011.

11. Cliff Kincaid, "Russian TV Sounds Like Soviet TV," *Accuracy in Media*, August 19, 2008, available from *www.aim.org/aim-column/russian-tv-sounds-like-soviet-tv/*, September 18, 2011.

12. *RT.com*, "RT watched more than other major international news channels in major cities," January 9, 2011, available from *rt.com/about/pressoffice/rt-watched-major-international-news-channels-major-u-s-cities/.*

13. *RT.com*, "RT in final of Monte Carlo TV Festival," May 17, 2011, available from *rt.com/about/pressoffice/rt-in-final-of-monte-carlo-tv-festival/*.

14. Heather A. Conley and Theodore P. Gerber *et al.*, "Russian Soft Power in the 21st Century: An Examination of Russian Compatriot Policy in Estonia," Washington, DC: Center for Strategic and International Studies (CSIS), August 2011, p. 12 (Sourced from Tatyana Kiilo and Yelena Vladimirova, "Compatriots," in *Russian Federation 2011: Short-term Prognosis*, ed., Karmo Tuur, Tartu, Estonia: Tartu University Press, 2011, p. 181.

15. Conley *et al.*, p. 14.

16. *Ibid.*

17. Andis Kudors, "'Russian World' — Russia's Soft Power Approach to Compatriots Policy," *Russian Analytical Digest*, Vol. 81, No. 10, June 16, 2010, pp. 2- 3, available from *kms1. isn.ethz.ch/serviceengine/Files/ISN/117631/ipublicationdocument_ singledocument/91db7fe2-59bf-46bb-8f89-fe8243377968/en/Russian_ Analytical_Digest_81.pdf*.

18. Conley *et al.*, p. 15.

19. Kudors, pp. 2- 3.

20. *Ibid.*, p. 3.

21. "Threats to Internet freedom in Russia, 2008, 2011," *AGORA Association*, June 2011, available from *www.openinform.ru/ fs/j_photos/openinform_314.pdf*.

22. John B. Dunlop, "Aleksandr Dugin's *Foundations of Geopolitics*," Princeton, NJ: Princeton University, available from *www. princeton.edu/~lisd/publications/wp_russiaseries_dunlop*.

23. Clare Lopez, "Book Review of Konstantin Preobrazhensky's *FSB's New Trojan Horse: Americans of Russian Descent*," *Gerard Group Intel Analysis*, June 10, 2009, available from *www. gerardgroup.com/newsletter/nl2009-06-10.php#Review*.

24. James Glazov, "Spies like Putin," *FrontPage Magazine*, July 8, 2010, available from *frontpagemag.com/2010/07/08/spies-like-putin-2/print/*.

25. *Ibid.*

26. Daniel Foggo and David Leppard, "Russian spy found in Commons; MP's aide arrested for spying," *The Sunday Times*, London, UK, December 5, 2010.

27. Report of the Attorney General to the Congress of the United States on the Administration of the Foreign Agents Registration Act, as amended, for the 6 months ending December 31, 2010, Washington, DC: U.S. Department of Justice, available from *www.fara.gov/reports/December31-2010.pdf*.

28. Taras Kuzio, "Russian Policy toward Ukraine during Elections," *Demokratizatsiya*, Vol. 15, No. 1, Winter 2005, p. 495-499.

29. Helle Dale, "Public Diplomacy 2.0: Where the U.S. Government Meets 'New Media'," *Heritage Foundation Backgrounder* No. 2346, December 8, 2009, available from *www.heritage.org/research/reports/2009/12/public-diplomacy-2-0-where-the-us-government-meets-new-media*.

30. Carnes Lord and Helle Dale, "Public Diplomacy and the Cold War: Lessons Learned," *Heritage Foundation Backgrounder* No. 2070, September 18, 2007, available from *www.heritage.org/research/reports/2007/09/public-diplomacy-and-the-cold-war-lessons-learned*.

31. Dale, "Public Diplomacy 2.0."

32. Judith McHale, Senate Foreign Relations Committee Confirmation Hearing, May 13, 2009, available from *www.state.gov/r/remarks/124155.htm*.

33. Dale, "Public Diplomacy 2.0."

34. Cohen and Dale, "Russian Anti-Americanism."

ABOUT THE CONTRIBUTORS

PAVEL K. BAEV is a Research professor at the Peace Research Institute, Oslo (PRIO), Norway, and Editor of *Security Dialogue*. After graduation from Moscow University in 1979, he worked in a research institute for the Union of Soviet Socialist Republics (USSR) Ministry of Defense. In 1988, Dr. Baev joined the newly created Institute of Europe within the Soviet Academy of Sciences. In autumn 1992, he took a sabbatical to move to PRIO where, from 1994 through 1996, Dr. Baev held a North Atlantic Treaty Organization (NATO) Democratic Institutions Fellowship. His recent books, *The Russian Army in a Time of Troubles* (1996) and *Russia's Policies in the Caucasus* (1997), are available from Sage Publications and the Brookings Institution, respectively.

STEPHEN J. BLANK has served as the Strategic Studies Institute's expert on the Soviet bloc and the post-Soviet world since 1989. Prior to that he was Associate Professor of Soviet Studies at the Center for Aerospace Doctrine, Research, and Education, Maxwell Air Force Base, AL; and taught at the University of Texas, San Antonio, and at the University of California, Riverside. Dr. Blank is the editor of *Imperial Decline: Russia's Changing Position in Asia*, coeditor of *Soviet Military and the Future*, and author of *The Sorcerer as Apprentice: Stalin's Commissariat of Nationalities, 1917-1924*. He has also written many articles and conference papers on Russia, the Commonwealth of Independent States, and Eastern European security issues. Dr. Blank's current research deals with proliferation and the revolution in military affairs, and energy and security in Eurasia. His two most recent books are *Russo-Chinese*

Energy Relations: Politics in Command, London, UK: Global Markets Briefing, 2006; and *Natural Allies? Regional Security in Asia and Prospects for Indo-American Strategic Cooperation*, Carlisle, PA: Strategic Studies Institute, U.S. Army War College, 2005. Dr. Blank holds a B.A. in history from the University of Pennsylvania, and an M.A. and Ph.D. in history from the University of Chicago.

ARIEL COHEN is Senior Research Fellow in Russian and Eurasian Studies and International Energy Policy at the Katherine and Shelby Cullom Davis Institute for International Policy at The Heritage Foundation in Washington, DC. He directs high-level conferences on Eurasian security, terrorism and energy; the rule of law, crime, and corruption; and a variety of other issues. He also directs Heritage's energy simulation exercises and war games involving Russia (2007-11). Dr. Cohen conducts White House briefings, and regularly lectures for the U.S. Government, including the Foreign Service Institute of the U.S. Department of State, the Joint Chiefs of Staff, and the Training and Doctrine and Special Forces Commands of the U.S. armed services, the Central Intelligence Agency, and the Defense Intelligence Agency. He frequently testifies before committees of the U.S. Congress, including the Senate and House Foreign Relations Committees, House Armed Services Committee, House Judiciary Committee and the Helsinki Commission. Dr. Cohen is also a Member of the Council of Foreign Relations and International Institute for Strategic Studies (London). Dr. Cohen authored *Russian Imperialism: Development and Crisis* (Praeger Publishers/Greenwood, 1996 and 1998), edited and co-authored *Eurasia in Balance* (Ashgate, United Kingdom, 2005), and authored

Kazakhstan: The Road to Independence: Energy Policy and the Birth of a Nation (School of Advanced International Studies, Johns Hopkins Central Asia Caucasus Institute, 2008). Dr. Cohen wishes to thank Robert Nicholson, a former Heritage Young Leaders program participant, for invaluable help in preparation of his chapter.

www.ingramcontent.com/pod-product-compliance
Lightning Source LLC
Chambersburg PA
CBHW052127270326
41930CB00012B/2795